Charles Chauncy

**The validity of Presbyterian Ordination asserted and maintained:**

A discourse delivered at the Anniversary Dudleian-Lecture, at Harvard College in Cambridge New England, May 12, 1762

Charles Chauncy

**The validity of Presbyterian Ordination asserted and maintained:**
*A discourse delivered at the Anniversary Dudleian-Lecture, at Harvard College in Cambridge New England, May 12, 1762*

ISBN/EAN: 9783337729882

Printed in Europe, USA, Canada, Australia, Japan

Cover: Foto ©ninafisch / pixelio.de

More available books at **www.hansebooks.com**

THE VALIDITY OF PRESBYTERIAN ORDINATION ASSERTED AND MAINTAINED.

A

# DISCOURSE

DELIVERED AT THE

ANNIVERSARY DUDLEIAN-LECTURE,

AT

HARVARD-COLLEGE IN CAMBRIDGE
NEW-ENGLAND,

MAY 12. 1762.

WITH AN APPENDIX,
GIVING a brief hiftorical account of the epiftles afcribed to IGNATIUS; and exhibiting fome of the many reafons, why they ought not to be depended on as his uncorrupted works.

BY CHARLES CHAUNCY, D. D.
ONE OF THE PASTORS OF THE FIRST CHURCH IN BOSTON.

---

BOSTON, NEW-ENGLAND:
PRINTED AND SOLD BY RICHARD DRAPER, IN NEWBURY-STREET, AND THOMAS LEVERETT IN CORNHILL. 1762.

THE words I would prefix to the following difcourfe, as a proper MOTTO, are thofe infpired ones of the apoftle PAUL,

" NEGLECT not the gift that is in thee,
" which was given thee by prophecy,
" with the laying on the hands of
" the prefbytery."

1 TIM. iv. 14.

THE honorable judge DUDLEY " ef-
" teem'd the method of ordination,
" as practifed in Scotland, at Gene-
" va, among the diffenters in England, and
" in the churches in this country, to be
" fafe, fcriptural and valid." And he firmly believed, " that the great head of the
" church, by his bleffed fpirit, had own'd,
" fanctified and bleft the adminiftration of
" gofpel ordinances by perfons ordained in
" this way; and that he would continue
" fo to do to the end of the world." I-

was accordingly his intention, that the discourse at this lecture should be adapted to the purpose of " explaining and maintaining " this kind of ordination. Not that he questioned " the validity of what is commonly called episcopal ordination, as performed in the church of England," or had it in his heart to encourage the saying any thing that would insinuate as tho' God had not blest, and would not go on to bless, the ministry of those who were thus ordained. Had none of the friends to ecclesiastical superiorities, according to the present episcopal form, been less wanting in candor and charity towards those who differ from them, we should never have heard of this lecture. It took rise, in the honorable founder's mind, from the narrow principles of those anathamatising zealots, who would confine salvation to their own church, by confining the validity of gospel ordinances to the administration of them by persons, upon whom the hands of a bishop, in their sense of the word, have been imposed. And he wisely ordered the preaching of it in this place, that our sons, who are sent here, from all parts of the land, to be trained up for public service, might be under advantage to hear and know the reasons, upon which they may, with all good conscience, join in communion with these churches,

and

and officiate as paftors in them, fhould they, when fitted for it, be called thereto in the providence of God.

You are, by this time, at no lofs to know the defign of the prefent difcourfe; that it is to vindicate the New-England churches in their method of ordination by prefbyters: or, in other words, to affert and maintain the fafety and validity of what is commonly called prefbyterian ordination, to the purpofes of the gofpel miniftry.

Only, before I come to the argument upon this head, it may not be amifs to mention a few things, in which we agree with our opponents.

We agree with them, it is the will of Chrift there fhould be officers in his church to preach the word, to adminifter the facraments, to exercife difcipline, and to commit thefe powers to other faithful men; and that this will of his extends to all ages, till time fhall be no more. "Lo, I am with you always, even to the end of the world." Whether it be his will, made known in the new-teftament-revelation, or elfe-where, that this work of the facred miniftry fhould be divided, and differently lodged in the hands of two diftinct orders of men, the one superior, the other inferior, we shall hear afterwards.

We agree with them, that none should take upon them the ministerial office, unless they are qualified for it conformably to the apostolic directions in the epistles to Timothy and Titus; and, if they are thus qualified, that they have no right to officiate as pastors in the church of Christ, till they are called hereto. " No man taketh this honor to himself, but he that is called of God as was Aaron." This call, in the opinion of the church of England, includes not only an ability given by God for the work of the ministry, but the excitement of an actual readiness in the persons who have it freely to devote themselves to the gospel service. We go farther, and add hereto, the voice of the church. And herein the advantage lies undeniably on our side, whether an appeal be made to scripture, or primitive antiquity. Even after the distinction between bishops and presbyters took place, it was by the suffrage of the people that this or that person was selected for this or the other cure. In this way, Alexander was chosen bishop of Jerusalem †; in the same way Fabianus was advanced to the see of Rome, upon the death of Anterus *,

as

† Euseb. Lib. 6. c. 11.   * Euseb. Lib. 6. c. 28.

as was also his successor Cornelius †; and it was by the same favor and suffrage of the people, " plebis favore, " § " populi suffragio," * that Cyprian was elected bishop of Carthage.—But instead of mispending the time to prove that which is so well known to all, in any measure acquainted with antiquity, it may rather be lamented, that the churches of Christ have so generally had wrested from them, in one way or another, this invaluable privilege. The people, constituting the episcopal church at home, scarce know what it is to have pastors of their own chusing. And the case is much the same with most of the protestant churches in Europe. The right of nomination is almost universally lodged, not with the people, but with princes or patrons, either clerical or secular, in consequence whereof their ministers are not of their own chusing, but such as others chuse for them. The New-England churches, blessed be God, possess and exercise the right of electing their pastors in the most ample manner of any in the whole christian world. May they ever " stand fast in this liberty " wherewith he who is " head over all things," has " made them free " ! And may their glory, in this respect, be never taken from them !

WE

† Cyprian. Epis. 67.  § Pontius in vita Cypriani.
\* Cyprian. Epis. 55. 40.

We agree with them, that, besides the call to, their muſt be an inveſtiture in, the miniſterial office, before perſons may, in ordinary caſes, regularly undertake to do the work that is proper to it: And we are further agreed, that ordination, meaning hereby impoſition of hands with ſolemn prayer, is the ſcripture-mode of this inveſtiture. By the uſe of this rite, with prayer, Paul and Barnabas were ſeparated to the work to which God had called them. So was Timothy; and ſo were thoſe ſeperated by him to the like work. And this has been the rite of miniſterial inveſtiture in uſe in the church all along from the beginning to this day.

Only, let it be remembered here, if, by ordination, our opponents ſuppoſe any moral gift, or ſpiritual power, inherent in the ordainers, is conveyed from them to the perſons upon whom they lay their hands, we beg leave to diſſent from them in this: Apprehending, and, as we judge, upon good grounds, that the authority of goſpel miniſters comes ſolely from Chriſt; while the ordainers are nothing more than his ſervants in inſtating the perſons they ordain in the regular exerciſe of this authority. As in the caſe of the mayor of a city, the kings charter of incorporation grants the power;
the

the burgesses and recorder only indigitate the proper recipient of it, and put him legally into the execution of his office. So here, Christ, in the gospel-charter, gives the power to act as his ministers; it only belongs to the ordainers to point out the persons with whom this power is intrusted, and regularly admit them to the exercise of it. The ordainers are to be considered, not as granting this power, but as acting ministerially in introducing capable persons, according to gospel-order, into the possession and use of it; the power itself having already been granted by Christ, the alone fountain of all power in the church, which is properly jure divino.

It follows from hence, as we judge, very obviously and justly, that those who are regularly vested with the ministerial office may fairly claim, and warrantably exercise, all the power that belongs to it, be the words of their investiture, or the intention of their ordainers, what they will. For as their office is from Christ his instituting will, not the intention or words of their ordainers, must be the true and only measure of their power.

In fine, we agree with our opponents, that the investiture by ordination must be the

the act of those, and only those, who are authorised to perform it. It is not left, in the sacred scriptures, a work common to all, and that may be done by any; but is the appropriate trust of some, in distinction from others. The brethren may not impose hands in consecrations to the gospel-ministry. Nothing occurs in the new-testament that can be construed to countenance such a practice. The business belongs to those only who are officers in the church of Christ; tho' not to these indiscriminately. For deacons, no more than mere brethren, may be allowed to lay on hands in ordination. The gospel officers who may do this are only those, who are authorised hereto; that is to say, they are only those whose office contains in it this, among other ministerial powers.

But who are these officers? This is the grand question: And the true answer to it will be decisive in the present dispute.

Our opponents say, bishops, considered as an order of men distinct from, and superior to, presbyters, are the only church-officers, who are vested with a right to ordain.

WE

We say, on the contrary, the scripture knows of no such order of officers in the church; and that gospel-presbyters, or such ministers of Christ as are allowed to have a right to preach the word, and administer the sacraments, are true scripture bishops, and cloathed with authority to do every thing that is to be done in the business of ordination.

And this is the point I am to make evident to you. In order whereto I might call your attention to those various arguments which have commonly been made use of upon like occasions with this; but, as I am confined within too narrow limits to do them proper justice, I shall wholly pass them over, though they carry in them, as I imagine, conclusive force, that I may leave room to enlarge on the following considerations, namely,

That the apostles of Christ, in settling the churches, constituted (besides the order of deacons) no more than one order of standing pastors; That these pastors, in their day, were called sometimes bishops, sometimes presbyters, and promiscuously pointed out by either of these names; and finally, that these bishops or presbyters were endowed with all the ordinary powers that

were

were to be exercised in the church of Christ, particularly with that of ordination.

These premises will, if set in a just point of light, unavoidably justify us in concluding, that presbyterian ordination, or, as it might with equal propriety be called, ordination by scripture-bishops, is safe and valid.

It scarce needs to be previously remark'd here, that the apostles, considered as such, were immediately sent by God, and this under the infallible guidance of inspiration, to preach the gospel to Gentiles as well as Jews, to gather churches in all parts of the world, and to appoint the officers, both for instruction and government, which were to be perpetuated in them for their edification in faith and holiness, till the time of the appearing of our Saviour to put an end to the present gospel-œconomy. This being taken for granted, I proceed to say,

That the apostles, in virtue of this plenitude of power, which they received immediately from Christ, constituted no more (besides the order of deacons, with which we have nothing to do at present) than one order of standing officers in the gospel-church. It is not my business, in this

this part of the difcourfe; to fay who thefe officers are: This will be done afterwards. At prefent I am concerned only with the fact itfelf; the proof of which is to be fetched from the facred writings. And the proof from hence is as full as could reafonably be defired.

NEITHER Chrift nor his apoftles have any where given inftructions, defcriptive of the perfons fit for the work of the miniftry, that are adapted to the fuppofition of a difference of order in the paftoral office. Had there been fuch a difference, different qualifications would have been requifite to the fuitable difcharge of the different trufts arifing therefrom; and it might juftly have been expected, that the fcriptures would have diftinguifhed between the qualifications refpectively proper for the management of each of thefe trufts. But they no where thus diftinguifh. They no where intimate, that fuch different endowments were neceffary. Far from this, they have fpecified the qualifications of one order of paftors only; as may be feen at large in the epiftles to Timothy and Titus. And what is ftrange, they have been very particular in difcribing the qualifications of this one order, while they are totally filent with refpect to the other that
is

is pleaded for, tho' that other is said to be by much the most honorable and important of the two.

In like manner, no rules are any where laid down for the guidance of ordainers in vesting ordinary ministers with different degrees of honor and power. They are no where told of the institution of two distinct orders of standing pastors; they are no where instructed to exercise their ordaining right conformably to this distinction, by placing some in an higher, others in a lower rank in the church. The sacred writings of the apostles say nothing to such a purpose as this. On the contrary, they present to our view a very full and explicit directory for the ordination of one order only of standing pastors. This we have in the Pauline instruction, referring to the settlement of the churches in Crete. The great apostle of the Gentiles gives it in charge to Titus, whom he left in this island with a direct view "to set in order the things that were wanting," to ordain fixed pastors in the several churches there. But what pastors were they? Of a different rank, some superior, others inferior? Not a word leading to such a tho't is to be found thro'-out his whole epistle. No; but the pastors he directs should be ordained were precisely of the fame rank or degree: Nor did Titus ordain any other. He could not indeed have done it, unlefs he had acted counter to the direction he had received from the infpired Paul.

The plea here is, Titus was himfelf, at this time, the fole bifhop of Crete, and as fuch entrufted with the power of ordaining inferior paftors. But this is a plea that can't be fupported upon juft and folid reafons; as we fhall have occafion, by and by, to make plain to you. In the mean time, we go on and fay further,

That, in the churches fettled in apoftolic times, no ordinary gofpel-minifters are to be found but of one order only. No other were in Lyftra, Iconium and Antioch. The apoftle Paul, with Barnabas, conftituted fuch paftors in all the churches in thefe places, but no other. Tis faid, * " they ordained elders," officers of one and the fame rank, "in every city." Should the words, χειροτονησαντες δε αυτοις πρεσβυτερους κατ᾽ εκκλησιαν, be rendered, not, " when they had ordained them elders in every city"; but, according to Dr. Hammond's † mind, " when they had ordain'd them elders church by church"; meaning, that a plurality of elders was conftituted in thefe churches collectively taken,

* Acts, xiv. 23. † Vid. Hammond in loc.

taken, not that there was this plurality in each individual church: I say, should this be allowed to be the sense of the words, it would notwithstanding remain the truth of fact, that one order of officers only was here spoken of; which is all I am at present proving from this text. Tho' I see not but a plurality of elders might be ordained "from church to church," in one church after another, and so in every church, as well as a single one in each church. And this is undoubtedly the true sense of the place, as it best accords with what was actually done in other churches.

At Ephesus, as in the place we have just been considering, no pastors had been settled but of equal degree. No other are mentioned by the apostle Paul, when he sent from Miletus to Ephesus to call to him the pastors of that church. He speaks of them in the stile of elders, ‡ evidently describing them as officers of one and the same rank. Had there been a bishop in this church, a single person of a superior order, to whom these elders were in subjection, 'tis strange he did not send for him likewise. Or if, at this time, he had been so far distant from his cure as not to be within call, it is equally strange he should say nothing relative to him; especially, as he was

‡ Acts, 20. 17.

was now to take his final leave of this church, § "knowing that they should see his face no more." This, if ever, was a fit season to mind them of their duty to their principal pastor. And it might the rather have been expected now, as he speaks of it as a thing known to him, ". that after his departure, grievous wolves would enter in among them, not sparing the flock." * Who so proper to have received instructions, in this case, as the chief shepherd? He tells them also, " that of their 'own selves men should arise, speaking perverse things to draw away disciples after them." ‡ And who so suitable to be charged with the care of withstanding these men as the bishop? And yet, the whole care of this church, now the apostle was going from them to return no more, he devolves on the elders; and this, tho' he knew they would be exposed to hazards, both from within themselves, and from abroad. This conduct is so unlike to the manner of after times, when bishops were advanced to superior dignity and power, that it must be supposed, either that the church of Ephesus had no such bishop, or that the apostle was strangely forgetful of him. Ignatius, a primitive father, who lived in this same century, if his epistles are genuine, as they are said to

B 2 be

§ Acts xx. Ver. 38. * Ver. 29. ‡ Ver. 30.

be by our opponents, did not treat the bishop of this, or any other of the churches he wrote to, with such neglect. He rather esteemed them officers so highly important as to make obedience to them an article worthy of his inculcation repeated to disgust. If the apostle Paul had been of the like spirit, he could not have omitted mentioning the bishop of Ephesus, if there had been one in the church there, in his day.

At Philippi likewise there were no fixt pastors but of one order. Very observable to this purpose is the inscription of the epistle to the church there. " To all the saints in Christ Jesus which are at Philippi, with the bishops and deacons." † Besides the deacons, no gospel pastors but of one order are here taken notice of. And the same silence runs thro' the epistle itself. These pastors, 'tis true, are called bishops; but they were bishops of the same class with the elders at Lystra, Iconium, Antioch and Ephesus. To be sure, they were not bishops in the sense of the church of England; and for this very good reason, because there was a plurality of them in this church at the same time; which flatly contradicts that essential article in the episcopal scheme, " one church one bishop."

No

† Philip. I. 1.

No pains have been wanting to evade this difficulty. Some, in order to it, have adopted the sense, the counterfeit Ambrose, but the true Hilary, would put upon the inscription, and read it thus, "Paul and Timothy, with the bishops and deacons, to the saints at Philippi." Should this construction be allowed to be just, it would not solve the difficulty. For it would still remain true, that there was a plurality of bishops in this church, unless it should be said, that these were the bishops, not of the church of Philippi, but of other churches happening to be there at this time; which is a meer random-conjecture, arbitrarily made without the least proof. But the construction itself is forc'd, and incapable of being justified. Should the inscriptions prefixt to the two epistles to the Corinthians be thus read and interpreted, no episcoparian, however zealous, would venture to say, we should have the true sense. And why any should pretend, that this is the sense of the inscription in dispute, no imaginable reason can be assign'd, setting aside that of serving an hypothesis; as the mode of diction is precisely the same in all these inscriptions. Besides, as some of the best critics have observed, if the apostle had intended to have taken in the bishops and deacons with him in saluting this church, he would

not

not have wrote, Παυλος και Τιμοθεος αγιοις τοις ουσιν εν Φιλιπποις, συν επισκοποις και διακονοις. I say, he would not have wrote thus, but Παυλος και Τιμοθεος, και οι συν έμοις επισκοποι και διακονοι, αγιοις τοις ουσιν εν Φιλιπποις. This was his mode of expression, when the brethren were co-partners with him in writing to the churches of Galatia. The form of words is,* Παυλος και οι συν έμοι παντες αδελφοι ταις εκκλησιαις της Γαλατιας. This same form of expression is used likewise by Polycarp, who had conversed with those who had seen our Lord, in his epistle to the Philippian church. † Πολικαρπος και οι συν αυτω πρεσβυτεροι to the church of God that sojourneth with the Philippians.—But this is too uncouth a sense to require any thing more to be said in confutation of it.

THE learned Dr. Hammond, to avoid the supposition of more bishops than one in this church, makes Philippi a metropolitan city, and the bishops of it, not the bishops of that single city only, but of the cities under that metropolis. § In answer whereto, Dr. Whitby assures us, ‡ that Philippi was not, at this time, a metropolitan city, but under the metropolis of Thessalonica, which was the metropolis of all Macedonia. And, as to its being a metropolitan church,

---

\* Gal. I. 1. 3.  † Inscription to Polycarp's epistle.
§ Hammond's note on Philip. I. 1.
‡ His note on Phillip. I. 1.

church, the learned bifhop Stillingfleet has abundantly prov'd, ‖ that there are no traces of it within the firft fix centuries. But it would be needlefs to enlarge here. The irreconcileablenefs of this notion with the ftate of things in apoftolic times is fo apparent, that the bare mentioning of it is enough to refute it. Dr. Maurice, tho' a ftrenuous advocate for diocefan epifcopacy, in oppofition to Mr. Clarkfon, fpeaks of this learned author, * as " alone " in this folution of the difficulty, and declines the defence of it; at the fame time, profeffing " that he could never find fufficient reafon to believe thefe bifhops any other than prefbyters, as the generality of the fathers, and of the church of England, have done." This is fairly and freely faid.

I shall only add here, the apoftle is as forgetful of the bifhop of this church, as he was of the bifhop of Ephefus ; for he takes no notice of any fingle paftor fuperior in rank to the other paftors. And the fame filence is obfervable in Polycarp's epiftle to this church a few years after. Will any pretend, that non-refidency was a common cuftom in thofe primitive times ? It is far more likely there were no fuch fuperior paftors, than that they fhould be thus abfent

‖ Irenicum page 359 &c.
\* " Defence of diocefan epifcopacy," page 27.

absent from their cures. And yet, this must have been the case, or it can't easily be accounted for, that no mention is made of them; especially when inferior pastors are applied to, and even the deacons are not neglected.

There is yet further evidence, that pastors of one order only were settled in the churches, in the first times of the gospel, from the apostle Peter's first epistle, which he directs to the christians * "scattered throughout Pontus, Galatia, Cappadocia; Asia, and Bythinia." Had this apostle been acquainted with any distinction of order between bishops and other pastors, he would undoubtedly have taken some notice of it in an epistle inscribed to christains in so many parts of the world. But, instead of this, he mentions only such pastors as were of equal rank; and these, while silent about others, he is express in urging to the faithful discharge of their duty as officers in the church of Christ. "The elders," says he, † "which are among you, I exhort, feed the flock of God."

And, from that apostolic injunction, ‡ " Is any sick among you? Let him call for the elders of the church, and let them pray over them": I say, from this apostolic rule, it
should

* 1. Peter I. 1. † 1. Pet. v. 1. 2. ‡ James v. 14.

should seem, that the then known ordinary pastors of the church were only elders. Why else are they particularly named, and christians instructed to apply to them to assist them with their prayers? Had there been, in those days, another and superior order of pastors, it cannot easily be supposed, they should have been wholly overlooked.—But I may not enlarge.

It is sufficiently evident, I would hope, from what has been offered, that the apostles of our Lord constituted no more than one order of standing pastors in the gospel-church. And so the way is prepared to show,

In the next place, that the names, bishop and presbyter, were, in apostolic times, reciprocal terms, and accordingly used as such to point out this constituted order of pastors. The texts to this purpose are full and strong. Thus, the elders, πρεσβυτεροι, whom the apostle Paul called to him from Ephesus, are applied to in the stile of overseers, επισκοποι. Having sent for them under the former name, he exhorts them under the latter. So we read, § " He sent to Ephesus, and called the elders, πρεσβυτερους, of the church; and when they were come to him, he said unto them — Take heed

§ Acts xx. 17, 28.

to the flock over which the Holy Ghost hath made you overseers," ἐπισκοπους. The same persons, who are stiled presbyters in one part of the same continued sentence, are in the other called bishops; and this, while spoken of in their proper character as officers of the church. In like manner, the apostle Peter promiscuously uses these names, applying them to the same pastors.\* " The elders (πρεσβυτερους) that are among you, I exhort — feed the flock of God, taking the oversight thereof, " ἐπισκοπουντες; acting the part, exercising the office, of bishops in it. The same promiscuous use is made of these names by the apostle Paul, in his epistle to Titus: For, having said some things descriptive of the qualifications of those he would have ordained elders, † πρεσβυτερους, he gives this as the reason of what he had offered, ‡ " a bishop, ἐπισκοπος, must be blameless —." There would be no connection, no force, in this reasoning, unless he meant by the names elders and bishops, πρεσβυτεροι and ἐπισκοποι, precisely the same church-officers.

It may not be amiss to observe here, for the sake of those who are so apt, in this dispute, to recur to antiquity, that both the greek and latin fathers, if we may believe
Dr.

---

\* 1 Pet. v. 1, 2.   † Tit. i. 5, 6.   ‡ Ver. 7.

Dr. Whitby,* an epifcoparian writer, "do with one confent declare, that bifhops were called prefbyters, and prefbyters bifhops, in apoftolic times, the names then being common. So Chryfoftom, Thodoret, Oecumenius and Theophylact, among the Greeks; and, among the Latins, Jerom, Pfeud-Ambrofius, Pelagius, and Primafius."

AND if the names were then common, and, as we have proved, promifcuoufly ufed to point out the fame church-officers, it is obvious, and yet juft to conclude, that thefe are the officers always intended, whether they are called bifhops or prefbyters. And upon the truth of this conclufion, we may warrantably affirm, that the bifhops, whofe qualifications are defcribed in the epiftle to Timothy, are precifely the fame with the elders Titus was directed to ordain in Crete; as alfo, that the bifhops of the church at Philippi were the fame with the elders fpoken of in other churches, and, è contra, the elders in other churches the fame with thefe bifhops. And in this view of the fcripture-language a perfect harmony runs thro' the whole new-teftament upon this head of ordinary paftors.

I

* Note on Philip. i. 1.

I SHALL finish this part of the discourse with the following remark, worthy of special notice, namely, that in all the above scripture-passages, the argument, in proof that bishops and presbyters are one and the same order of pastors, is not grounded meerly on the promiscuous use of these names, but their being so used as to point out the work, or describe the qualifications, that are proper to one and the same office. Perhaps, the argument would have been valid, could we have reasoned only from the reciprocal use of these names; but, as we reason not meerly from this, but from the appropriation also of the same work, and the same moral endowments, to the same persons under these different names, the arguing is unexceptionably strong and conclusive. And so it is confessed to be by some of the best writers in favor of episcopacy, particularly by the late celebrated bishop Hoadly, who, far from calling in question the strength of this way of arguing, acknowledges it's force, * and pleads, that the bishops of the church of England don't answer to those that are promiscuously called either bishops or presbyters in the new-testament, but to officers superior to them: A suggestion we shall have opportunity afterwards to consider. But, previous to

* "Reasonableness of conformity to the church of England." page 388, 389, &c.

to this, we shall go on to the last branch of the present argument, and say,

THAT these officers of equal rank, who are promiscuously called either bishops or presbyters, were endowed with all the ordinary powers proper to be exercised in the church of Christ, with that of ordination, as well as those of teaching, baptising and administering the Lord's supper.

THAT they were authorised to preach and administer the sacraments, our opponents do freely allow. And from hence it might be consequentially argued, à fortiori, that they were empowered also to ordain. For these are ministerial acts more excellent and important in their nature, than that of ordination. — But the limits to which I am confined oblige me to pass over this argument.

IT is also allowed, and even insisted on, by episcopal writers, that the same persons who are authorised to govern, are in like manner, empowered to ordain. Now, it were easy to show, from the scriptures, that the former of these powers was given to presbyters; from whence it might be inferred, that they were vested with the latter. But this argument also I shall dismiss,

miss, that I may have time more fully to lay before you the direct proof we have, that the power of ordination was lodged with ordinary pastors or presbyters.

AND we prove this from scripture-instances of this kind of ordination.

IF the sacred books of the new-testament present to our view examples of ordination by presbyters, we shall take it for granted, this will be esteemed a good reason why we should think, they were vested with ordaining power; and that presbyters now will act warrantably, while they copy after the pattern that is set them in the inspired writings. It only remains therefore to produce these instances.

THE first is that of the separation of Barnabas and Paul to the work to which God had called them; the account whereof is recorded * in these words, " There were in the church that was at Antioch certain prophets and teachers.—As they ministred to the Lord, and fasted, the holy Ghost said, separate me Barnabas and Paul to the work whereunto I have called them. And when they had fasted and prayed, and laid hands on them, they sent them away." This is the most circumstantial account
given

* Acts xiii. 1, 2, 3.

given in fcripture of an ordination. The perfons ordained were previoufly called of God; they were fet apart to the fpecial work to which they had been called; all the minifterial acts any where mentioned, in the new-teftament, as accompanying the feparation of perfons to the fervice of the church of Chrift, were performed, impofition of hands, fafting and prayer; and what is more directly to our purpofe, the ordainers were " the prophets and teachers" of the church at Antioch. Thefe teachers were its ordinary paftors, the fame officers that are elfewhere promifcuoufly called bifhops or prefbyters. Moft certainly, they could not be bifhops, in the fenfe of the church of England, becaufe there was a plurality of them in this church. What more can be wanting to make this a compleat inftance in our favor?

The objections againft it only ferve as fo many occafions to place it in a ftronger point of light.

'Tis faid, by Turrianus, bifhop Bilfon, and fome others, that this feparation of Barnabas and Paul was the act, not of the teachers, but of the prophets (extraordinary officers) who impofed hands with them. But this is only faid, not proved; nor can

it

it be proved. The divine order, "separate me Barnabas and Paul," was as truly directed to these teachers, as to the prophets; they as certainly laid hands on these persons, and prayed over them, in separating them to their work; and as much is attributed to them, relative to their separation, as to the prophets. And consequently, if it can be argued, from any thing that is here said to these prophets, or that is spoken of as done by them, that they were vested with the power of ordination; it may, in the same way, and with equal strength, be argued, that the teachers also were endowed with the same power; for there is nothing said to the prophets, but what is equally said to the teachers; nor was any thing done by the former, but the same was done by the latter.

It is pleaded, by the whole body of episcopal writers, that Barnabas and Paul were, before this, commissioned ministers of Christ; and that their present separation was only to a special service among the Gentiles. It is acknowledged; but, at the same time, denied that this makes any real alteration in the case. For it is to be remembred, the thing intended by ordination is not, that the ordainers should commission persons to do the work of the ministry.

ſtry. This is done by Chriſt. It only belongs to them to declare who theſe perſons are, and ſeparate them to the work to which Chriſt has commiſſioned them. They don't make them miniſters; but, being authoriſed hereto, give them an authentic character as ſuch in the eye of the world. They don't confer upon them their authority in the goſpel-kingdom; but let them into the exerciſe of the authority proper to their office, with the ſolemnity the ſcripture eſteems regular and decent. And it might ſeem good to the holy Ghoſt to order, that Barnabas and Paul, tho' before commiſſioned and ſent by Chriſt, ſhould yet, at this time, be ſeparated to their work by man, in the common and ordinary way. Neither of them, from any thing ſaid of the matter in the ſacred books, appear to have been thus ſeparated before now; and as they were now ſeparated to the work to which they had been called by impoſition of hands, with faſting and prayer, it may with all reaſon be affirmed, that this ſeparation was a true ſcripture-ordination. All the outward actions common to an ordination were performed upon this occaſion, and particularly that of laying on of hands. They were, in a word, ſeparated to the ſervice aſſigned them in the ſame way that Timothy was ſeparated to the miniſterial work,

work, and afterwards feparated others to it; in the fame way Titus was directed to ordain elders in the churches at Crete; yea, in the fame way they themfelves ordained elders at Lyftra, Iconium, and Antioch in Pifidia, and this, while upon the very fervice they were now feparated to. And why their feparation, at this time, fhould not be efteemed as proper a fcripture-ordination as their's, which was effected by the performance of the fame outward actions, no better reafon can be given, than that it will not fall in with the fcheme of our opponents.

It is further objected, this feparation of Barnabas and Paul was in confequence of an immediate order from the holy Ghoft, and therefore a precedent not pleadable but in like circumftances. The anfwer is obvious. Both Timothy and Titus were immediately directed by an apoftle of Jefus Chrift, fpeaking to them under the infpiration of the holy Ghoft, to ordain paftors at Ephefus and Crete; and yet, the objectors themfelves plead thefe inftances in fupport of the right of bifhops, in their fenfe of the word, to ordain; and this, to the exclufion of prefbyters. And if the plea is good on their fide, it is equally fo on our's. I would fay further, this objection, inftead of fetting afide the inftance before us as a precedent, makes

makes it the more ſtrongly valid. For it cannot be ſuppoſed, if ordinary teachers were unſuitable church-officers to perform the buſineſs of ordination, that the holy Ghoſt would have ordered them to do it. And, by his committing this work to them, we have an authentic precept, as well as example, for ordination by common teachers, ſtanding ordinary paſtors of the churches. And let me add here, it is highly probable, this direction from the holy Ghoſt, giving riſe to this inſtance of ordination by ordinary teachers, was intended for a precedent to the Gentile churches in all after times. This was the judgment of the learned Dr. Lightfoot. " No better reaſon, ſays he\*, can be given of this preſent action, than that the Lord did hereby ſet down a platform of ordaining miniſters to the church of the Gentiles in future times. "

ANOTHER inſtance to our purpoſe we have in the caſe of Timothy, who was ſeparated to the goſpel-miniſtry with the laying on of the hands of the preſbytery ; as is evident from that exhortation of the apoſtle Paul addreſſed to him, in my text, " Neglect not the gift that is in thee, which was given thee by prophecy, with the laying on of the hands of the preſbytery : " The meaning

\* Vol. I. page 189.

meaning of which words, compared with what is said upon the matter in 2 Tim. i. 6. may, I think, be fully expressed in the following paraphrase, " Improve the gift of the holy Ghost, which I imparted to you in an extraordinary measure, according to the prophesies which went before concerning you, when you was separated to the work of the ministry with the laying on of the hands of the consistory of presbyters."

You observe, I do not interpret the gift here said to be in Timothy of his office as a minister, but of the communication of the holy Ghost, in an extraordinary manner qualifying him for it; which appears to me the most easy and natural sense. You observe likewise, I speak of this gift of the holy Ghost as imparted to Timothy, thro' the hands of the apostle Paul, not the hands of the presbytery. There is no certain example of such a communication to be met with in the new-testament. Perhaps, the holy Ghost, in the days of the apostles, was never imparted thro' any hands but those of an apostle. But should it have been otherwise, this was the way of communication in the present case. For the apostle Paul expressly speaks of this gift * as a gift that was in Timothy " by the putting on of his hands." These presbyters therefore did not

* 2 Tim. i. 6.

not impose hands on Timothy with a view to communicate to him this gift. It was imparted wholly thro' the hands of the apostle Paul. And yet, the presbytery as certainly imposed their hands on Timothy as Paul imposed his. And why? No good reason can be assigned for it but this, that they might separate him to the gospel-ministry in the ordinary way, by using the scripture-rite common upon such an occasion. And if it be supposed, that this gift of the holy Ghost was imparted to Timothy thro' the hands of Paul, about the time that he was separated to the ministry by the laying on of the hands of the concessus of presbyters, we shall have an easy and consistent sense of this whole affair.

The truth of the case seems plainly to be this. The apostle Paul imposed his hands on Timothy to communicate to him the gift of the holy Ghost; and either with the apostle, or, as I rather think, afterwards, the council of presbyters laid on their's, separating him, by this rite, to his work, as Paul himself, with Barnabas, some time before, had been separated to their's. And very observable, it may be proper to remark here, is the analogy between this separation of Timothy, and that of Paul and Barnabas. They were separated by express direction

direction from the holy Ghost; so was Timothy, for he was pointed out by prophecy, that is, by holy men prophetically speaking of him by inspiration of the holy Ghost, as a fit person to be employed in the service of the gospel. And it was probably owing to this, that he was so soon separated to this work, being, at this time, a very young man, and in danger, on that account, of being despised. They were seperated also by the laying on of the hands of the prophets and teachers, that is, the ordinary pastors of the church at Antioch; so was Timothy, by the laying on of the hands of the company of presbyters, residing where he now was.

But the pertinency of this instance will appear with a brighter lustre, by considering the objections that are made to it; as, by this means, we shall have an opportunity of going more critically into the examination of it.

It is objected, the word presbytery, πρεσβυτεριου, here used, means the office ordained to, not the consistory of ordaining presbyters. This was Calvin's interpretation, when he wrote his institutions *; tho'

---
* Says he, "Quod de impositione manuum presbyterii dicitur, non ita accipio quasi Paulus de seniorum collegio loquatur; sed hoc nomine ordinationem ipsam intelligo" ——.
Institut. lib. 4. cap. 3. sect. 16.

tho' afterwards, in his commentary upon this text, having attained to greater maturity of judgment, he fell in with the commonly received sense ‡. The other, by whomsoever it is given, will exhibit a down-right piece of nonsense, unless the substantive πρεσβυτεριου is made the genitive case, not to the immediately foregoing word χειρων, but to that far distant one χαρισματος; and the text be accordingly read, " Neglect not the gift of the presbyteratus which was given thee by the laying on of hands." But this grammatical transposition is arbitrary beyond all reasonable bounds. And should the like liberty be taken in other cases, we might make the scripture speak, in any place, just what we please. Besides, the word πρεσβυτεριον is never used in this sense in the new-testament; but always as signifying " concessus, senatus presbyterorum." This also is it's meaning in the writings of the fathers, as may be seen in the famous Blondell's " apologia pro sententia Hyeronimi." † And this is its meaning particularly in Ignatius's epistles, whose authority will not be questioned by those we are at present concerned with. He often uses this word, and never in any other sense.

But

---

‡ " Presbyterium.] Qui hic collectivum nomen esse putant, pro collegio presbyterorum positum, recte sentiunt meo judicio." In loc.

† Page 89, 90.

But should we allow this pretended sense of the word to be the true one, and, in consequence hereof, that Timothy was ordained, not by an assembly of presbyters, but to the degree of the presbyterate; instead of helping the cause of our opponents, it would, unluckily for them, very much serve our's. For Timothy, according to this interpretation, was, at the time, when this epistle was wrote, nothing more than a presbyter, whatever he might be afterwards: And yet, he is particularly apply'd to, in the epistle itself, as one intrusted with the power of ordination, and accordingly instructed to use caution and prudence in the management of this trust, "not suddenly laying hands on any man." And if Timothy, while a meer presbyter, was spoken of, by an inspired apostle, as one vested with ordaining power, it is as good a proof of the power we are establishing, as if he was ordained by a consistory of presbyters.

'Tis again said, by the presbytery here is intended, not an assembly of presbyters, but the college of apostles. So speak Chrysostom, Theophilus, Theodoret, Oecumenius, and after them such learned men as Dr. Hammond, Mr. Drury, and some others; but, as we imagine, without any sufficient reason to support this sense of the word.

word. It is indeed a sense that carries with it not the least probability of truth. The apostle Peter, 'tis true, introduces an exhortation to Presbyters, by taking to himself the stile of a fellow-presbyter, συν-πρεσβυτερος * ; but the apostles, in a collective view, are never once spoken of, in the new-testament, as a presbytery; nor is the word, πρεσβυτεριον, ever used by any ancient writer (as Mr. Boyse observes) to signify the bench of apostles. Far from this, when met together in council at Jerusalem, upon a special occasion, with the elders; they are carefully and particularly distinguished from them, every time they are mentioned.‡ Nor can it well be imagined, if the other apostles had joined with Paul in laying their hands on Timothy, either for imparting the holy Ghost, or separating him to the gospel-ministry, that this humble apostle would have omitted mentioning their names, since he so expressly mentions his own. Besides, there is not the least reason to think, that either all, or most, or any considerable number of the apostles were together at this time. 'Tis far more likely, from the history we have in the acts of their travels, and dispersions from each other, that Paul only was now present, and that the presbytery that laid their hands on Timothy was not the company of apostles, but such presbyters

---

* 1 Pet. v. 1.  ‡ Acts xvth chap.

presbyters as they had conftituted in the feveral churches.

But fhould it be fuppofed, that the apoftles were now together, and that this prefbytery was the affembly of apoftles, it would be of no real fervice to the epifcopal caufe. For 'tis plain, they acted not, in their apoftolical character, but as presbyters. Why elfe are they called a presbytery? It cannot reafonably be thought, if the holy Ghoft intended to declare, in this text, that Timothy was ordained by apoftolical authority, and not that which is vefted in prefbyters, he would fo exprefsly have fpoken of the apoftles as acting in this affair as a presbytery. It fhould rather feem evident from hence, that the work they now did was common and ordinary, and fuch as might be done by thefe officers, under whofe ftyle they are reprefented as performing this action.

Finally, it is pleaded, that Timothy was vefted with his office by the laying on of the apoftle Paul's hands, while the confiftory of presbyters, by impofing their's, only gave their concurring approbation. And for the proof of this we are turned to 2 Tim. i. 6. where Paul, calling upon Timothy "to ftir up the gift that was in him," adds,

adds, "which is in thee by the putting on of my hands."

THE answer is easy. This same apostle attributes as much to the hands of the presbytery in 1 Tim. 4. 14, as he does to his own hands in the place referred to in his second epistle; and consequently there is just the same reason to say, that the presbytery ordained Timothy, as that Paul ordained him. Besides, it cannot be reasonably supposed, that an inspired apostle should permit a number of presbyters to join with him in the sacred solemnity of imposing hands, if they had not a right, as officers in the church of Christ, to perform this action; and their performing it is a sure argument of their right to do the thing intended by it, that is, to separate a person to the work of the gospel-ministry: As they that have a right to apply water in the name of the Father, and the Son, and the holy Ghost, have a right to baptise; and they that have a right to set apart bread and wine, and distribute it to the people, have a right to administer the Lord's supper.

BUT the truth of the matter is, it is far from being evident, that Paul imposed hands with the presbytery in Timothy's ordination; and I am strongly inclined to think

think he did not. The gift the apostle speaks of, in his second epistle to Timothy, which, says he, "is in thee by the putting on of my hands," was undoubtedly the gift of the holy Ghost in miraculous powers; but whatever the gift was, it was imparted by the apostle's own hands. Not a word is said of the presbytery, or any person whatever, as joining with him, not so much as in a way of concurring approbation. Whereas, in the passage we are now considering, recorded in the first epistle, the thing that was done, whatever it was, was done with the laying on of the hands of the presbytery. Their hands only are mentioned, not a word is drop'd insinuating that Paul's hands were joined with their's. It is therefore highly probable, if not certain, that Paul imposed hands on Timothy to confer the gift of the holy Ghost, which was usually, if not always, done by some apostle in this way; and that the presbytery afterwards laid on their hands for another purpose, that of separating him to the work of the ministry, which also was usually done in this way.

Or if it should be still said, that Paul laid hands on Timothy at the same time the presbytery imposed their's, he did it principally that through his hands, being an apostle, the holy Ghost might be imparted

to

to him; they, that he might, in the ordinary method, be separated to the gospel-ministry. So that, in either of these ways, we have an evident instance of ordination by presbyters. In the former, they were sole ordainers; in the latter, ordainers in partnership with the apostle Paul.

I can't help saying here, if, instead of, "the laying on of the hands of the presbytery," it had been wrote, "the laying on of the hands of the episcopate," our opponents would have triumphed in having an unexceptionable instance of episcopal ordination. But this occasion of glorying is happily taken away. And it is remarkable, tho' we have examples, in scripture, of ordination by both extraordinary and ordinary officers, by apostles, by prophets, by evangelists, by teachers or common pastors and presbyters; yet we no where read of an ordination by any person under the name of a bishop. There is a total silence throughout the new-testament upon this head. This observation, to use the words of your worthy Divinity-professor, in a book of his, relative to this controversy, wrote near 40 years ago, entitled, "sober remarks," and which I would recommend to your diligent perusal, "This observation, says he,\* " may perhaps draw
"some

\* Page 115.

"some weak persons into doubts about the
"validity of episcopal ordination.—But the
"truth of the case is, that bishops and
"presbyters are one and the same order by
"divine institution; and that they succeed
"the apostles, in all their ordinary
"powers, of which that of ordination is
"one; which is warrant enough for ordi-
"nation by presbyters, and the very same
"warrant which those have for it, who
"are now, by custom and human consti-
"tution, dignified and distinguished with
"the title of bishops."

I HAVE now considered the argument at first proposed, in all its parts. And the sum of what has been said, that we may have it in one view, is this; that the apostles of Christ, in consequence of their commission from him, and as acting under the inspiration of the holy Ghost, constituted and settled in the church, besides the order of deacons, no more than one order of fixed pastors; that they promiscuously point out the pastors of this one order by the names bishop and presbyter, sometimes using the former, sometimes the latter, and meaning by either precisely these pastors of one and the same order; and finally that they give us abundant reason to believe, that these pastors of this one order were

endowed

endowed particularly with the power of ordination, inſtances whereof they have left upon ſacred record. The concluſion from which premiſes, if they have been clearly and fully evidenced to be true, as I truſt they have, is unqueſtionably this, that ordination by presbyters, according to the uſual method in theſe churches, is ſafe and valid, becauſe agreeable to the holy ſcriptures, and warranted by them.

But notwithſtanding all that has been offered in proof of the point we have been upon, it ought not, it is acknowledged, to be received as truth, unleſs the contrary evidence can fairly be ſet aſide. This therefore makes it neceſſary to conſider what is pleaded on the other ſide of the queſtion. And this I ſhall now do, giving what is ſaid its full ſtrength, ſo far as I am able. For if the counter-evidence, in it's full weight, will not admit of a juſt and ſolid anſwer, we ought, in all reaſon, to eſteem the above proof to be defective, how plauſible ſoever it may appear in a ſeparate view.

The firſt thing ſaid in favor of the ſuperiority of biſhops to presbyters, and in vindication of their claim to the powers of ordination and government is, that they
are

are succeffors to the apoftles, and derive from them this fuperiority of order and power.

THE anfwer is ready. The apoftles, as fuch, were extraordinary officers, and had no succeffors. They received their commiffion immediately from Chrift, their charge was unlimited, their province the whole world. They were, by office, the teachers of all nations, had power to gather churches every where, to fettle them with proper officers, to infpect over them, and give binding rules and orders for the good government of them; and all this, under the infallible guidance of the holy Ghoft. It will not be pretended, I truft, that bifhops, in thefe refpects, are succeffors to the apoftles. In their proper apoftolic character, they were far exalted above all bifhops. As the great Dr. Barrow expreffes it, (to adapt his words to the prefent cafe) " It would be a difparagement to an apof- " tle to take upon him the bifhoprick of " Rome; as it would be to the king, to " become mayor of London; or to the bi- " fhop of London, to become vicar of Pan- " crafs." The apoftolic office, as fuch, was perfonal and temporary; not succeffive and communicable: Neither did the apoftles communicate it. Thofe parts indeed

deed of their office which were ordinary, and intended for perpetual use, such as feeding the church of God with the word and sacraments, and restraining them within the rules of good order, were communicated from them to others. We have accordingly seen, that they appointed standing pastors in the churches, vesting them with all the powers proper for the work of the ministry, for the edifying the body of Christ. And in a lax sense, these may be called successors to the apostles, as having derived their power from them in Christ's name. And in this loose sense only may bishops be said to be successors to the apostles. They certainly do not succeed them in their office, considered as apostolic; but in such powers of it only as are ordinary and communicable. And here they are perfectly upon a par with common pastors or presbyters, unless it can be proved, that the apostles in communicating these powers, made a difference, committing some to a superior order called bishops, and others to an inferior one described by the name of presbyters. This is what we may reasonably expect to see evidenced. The new-testament is open. If it contains any such evidence, let it be produced. We imagine it contains clear evidence of the contrary, and that we have given such evidence. Meerly the cal-

F ling

ling bishops successors to the apostles won't prove their superiority; tho', by the way, they are never so called in the sacred books. And should it be allowed, that the fathers, in after times, speak of them in this stile, it can be in a loose sense only; meaning, that apostolic power had been communicated to them, tho' what that power was, can never be determined meerly by their being called the apostles successors. The bible only can settle this point.

It is further said, in defence of the episcopal scheme, that Timothy and Titus were bishops, the one of Ephesus, the other of Crete, meaning hereby officers of a rank superior to the other pastors of the churches in those places, with whom, as such, were lodged the powers of ordination and jurisdiction.

'Tis reply'd, they are neither of them called bishops any where in the new-testament. This name, 'tis true, is given them in the postscripts to the epistles that are directed to them. But I need not say, that these postscripts are after-additions, and not very ancient ones neither. This is sufficiently known to all men of learning, who accordingly lay no stress upon them. 'Tis true likewise, that they are called bishops,

the

the one of Ephesus, the other of Crete, by the fathers; but not by the more primitive ones. Dr. Whitby honestly confesses, ‡ that "he could not find, within the three first centuries, any intimations that they bore this name." He adds indeed, "this defect is abundantly supplyed by the concurrent suffrage of the 4th and 5th centuries." But these were times too far distant from Timothy and Titus to be rely'd on for the truth of this fact; especially, as, in these times, they had greatly departed from the simplicity of the gospel. And 'tis observable, Eusebius, the great source of primitive ecclesiastical history, only says, "it is reported," ιστορειται * dicitur, "that Timothy was bishop of Ephesus, and Titus bishop of Crete." And he has himself taught us, how far we may depend upon this report, by what he tells us a little before, § "that he could trace no foot-steps of others going before him, only in a few narratives." And the suffrage of these centuries is the less to be regarded, in this particular, because it does not agree with the scripture-account of Timothy and Titus. Timothy is expresly called "an evangelist," 2 Tim. iv. 6. And his work, as such, was inconsistent with his being the bishop of Ephesus, or any other church. The business of

‡ Preface to the epistle to Titus.   * Lib. III. cap. 4.
§ Lib. I. cap. 1.

an evangelift, as Eufebius ‡ juftly reprefents it, was, " to lay the foundation of faith in ftrange nations, to conftitute them paftors; and, having committed to them the cultivating thofe new plantations, to pafs on to other countries and nations." And this defcription of evangelifts perfectly agrees with what the fcripture fays both of Timothy and Titus. They evidently appear to have been itinerant miffionaries, not fettled paftors. To be fure, they fuftained no fixed relation to the churches of Ephefus and Crete, and confequently were not the bifhops of them; for they continually went about from place to place, as the fervice of the churches made it neceffary, and were as long, and it may be longer, in other churches than thofe that are faid to be their fettled charge. And would any man, as Mr. Boyfe expreffes it,† " call him the fixt bifhop of London that fhould only perform the epifcopal functions there for a year or two, but for twenty or thirty years is found to perform the fame epifcopal functions in moft other diocefes of England, nay in many diocefes in France, Spain and Italy?" Can fuch an itinerary miniftry as this confift with a man's fixt relation to a particular church, which enjoys no more of his labors and care than twenty or thirty churches more? BUT

‡ Lib. III. cap. 37.
† " Account of the ancient epifcopacy," page 331.

But the strength of the argument from Timothy and Titus chiefly lies in this, that they were charged with the management of ordination at Ephesus and Crete. Titus particularly was left in Crete with a professed view to his ordaining elders in the cities there. The answer is, it will not from hence follow, that they were vested with an exclusive power of ordination. I argue upon the matter thus ; either elders had been settled before this in the churches at Ephesus and Crete, or they had not ; and whether our opponents proceed upon the former, or latter of these suppositions, their reasoning is inconclusive.

If elders had been settled in these churches, the consequence is far from being just, Timothy and Titus were particularly entrusted with the affair of ordination in these churches, therefore the power was in them exclusive of the standing pastors. By this way of arguing, they must have been sole preachers, as well as ordainers ; for they are as particularly charged to do the work of preaching, as that of ordaining. And by this same method of reasoning, the church of Rome must be justified in their plea for Peter's supremacy ; for there are not wanting texts of scripture, in which he is particularly apply'd to, and charged with

instructions

inſtructions and orders without mentioning the other apoſtles. The plain truth is, as theſe evangeliſts were aſſiſtants to the apoſtles, and left in thoſe churches extraordinarily qualified to ſupply their place, it was proper they ſhould have particularly committed to them the chief management of ordination, and all other affairs pertaining to the kingdom of Chriſt, while they continued among them. But how does this prove, that, when they were gone, as was ſoon the caſe, this ſame work might not be done by the ſtanding paſtors? Or that the ſtanding paſtors might not, or that they did not, join with them in doing it, while they were actually preſent? 'Tis far more probable that they did, than that they did not. Timothy's ordination by the confiſtory of presbyters would naturally put him upon going into the like practice. To be ſure, ſome poſitive good evidence ought to be given, that he did not, and that the power of ordination was ſolely and excluſively veſted in him.

THE other ſuppoſition was that of there being no ſettled paſtors in theſe churches, when theſe inſtructions were given to Timothy and Titus. And in this view of the fact, I ſee not but the diſpute muſt be at once ended; for their being directed to ordain

dain paftors in churches that as yet had none, can't poffibly prove, that thefe paftors, when ordained, might not ordain others alfo. And perhaps this is the real truth of the cafe. I am well affured, it will be found, upon trial, to be an infuperable tafk to make it appear, that either of thefe churches, at this time, were fettled with paftors. They were, moft probably, in the fame imperfect ftate with the churches of Lyftra, Iconium, and Antioch, before Barnabas and Paul, upon their return to them, ordained them elders. And, it may be, as Dr. Benfon well obferves, * moft of the churches the apoftle Paul writes to were in the fame imperfect unfettled ftate, at the time when he wrote to them.

I SHALL only add here, as Timothy and Titus were evangelifts, they had no fuccefsors; or if they had, fixed bifhops could not be their fucceffors. Nor will it follow, becaufe thefe evangelifts were left at Ephefus and Crete to manage the affair of ordination, that therefore bifhops, any more than prefbyters, have this power. It muft firft be proved, and upon the foot of good evidence, that bifhops, meaning hereby officers in the church fuperior to prefbyters, were fixed

---

\* Effay at the end of his paraphrafe and note on the epiftle of Paul to Timothy, page 80.

ed in thefe places, and that the ordaining power was lodged with them, to the exclufion of presbyters; which has never yet been done, and I am fully perfuaded never will.

It is pleaded yet further, that the angels of the feven Afian churches, in the book of the Revelation, were bifhops; that is, fuch bifhops as the prefent argument is concerned with, or they are mentioned to no purpofe. But how does it appear, that thefe angels were bifhops in this fenfe? If the word is here ufed collectively, meaning the paftors of thefe churches, and not a fingle one in each church, the argument is at once fuperfeded. And it ought to be thus underftood. Such an expofition beft agrees with the manner of fpeaking thro'-out this whole book, in which like words are commonly ufed in this collective fenfe. Nor, unlefs the word is thus interpreted, will the other paftors of thefe churches have any concern in the meffages that are fent to the churches, which it would be highly unreafonable to fuppofe. But, if every one of thefe angels fhould be allowed to mean a fingle perfon, how will it follow herefrom, that they were bifhops vefted with the fole power of ordination and government in thefe churches? The word angel

carries

carries in it's meaning nothing that imports this; nor is there any thing said, in the epistles themselves, from whence it can be deduced. The argument therefore must be wholly grounded on this, that these angels are singled out, and particularly wrote to. But this they might be, supposing there was no greater distinction between them and the other pastors, than between Peter and the other apostles; between rectors and curates; between an assembly of equal ministers and their præses. In short, it must be proved by other evidence than what is contained in the word angel, or the application of this word to a single person, if proved at all, that bishops were hereby intended, meaning by bishops officers in these churches endowed with the sole power of ordination and government; which evidence has never yet been produced.

THE last plea, and that which is triumphed in as decisive, is the suffrage of all antiquity in favor of bishops, as an order of men in the church superior to presbyters, to whom belonged the powers of ordination and government.

BUT, before I come to this plea, it may be proper just to observe, that we are now disputing

disputing against the episcopal scheme, and particularly that branch of it, the confining ordination to bishops, not as a meer ecclesiastical appointment, [a prudential expedient; but as an institution of Jesus Christ, and an institution of his essentially connected with the validity of gospel-administrations. And in this view of the matter, the demand, we imagine, is highly reasonable, "what saith the scripture?" It is to little purpose to tell us of the fathers, and that it is uninterruptedly handed down from them as a fact, that bishops were superior to presbyters, and had the sole right of ordination. This cannot make episcopal-ordination necessary to the validity of gospel-ordinances. It must be constituted necessary, if so at all, by the revelations of God, and in fair and legible characters too. We may, with all reason, expect to find both the constitution itself, and it's necessity, delivered in the sacred books, not by innuendoes, far-fetch'd arguments, or probable conjectures; but with so much positive clearness, and express affirmation, as to leave no reasonable room for doubt. And there would now be no need of testimonies from the fathers. It would indeed be dishonorary to the sacred scriptures, and a gross reflection on them as not being a perfect and sufficient rule, if we might not, without traditionary helps from the

the elders, depend on them for the essentials of salvation. And, considering the sentiments of our Saviour concerning the traditions handed down to the Jews from their elders, this kind of tradition seems to be one of the last things suitable to be recurred to, in order to our knowing what is necessarily connected with true christianity.

Having remark'd this, I come to consider the plea that is so much gloried in, as carrying with it even demonstration. And, that it might lose none of it's strength, I shall give it you in the words of the celebrated bishop Hoadly, who has wrote, perhaps, in as masterly a way, upon this side of the controversy, as any who have handled it. In his book entitled, " The reasonableness of conformity to the church of England, " in order to prove, " that the apostles left the power of ordaining presbyters in the hands of fix'd bishops, " he says,*
" This being a matter of fact, past many
" ages ago, the only method by which
" we can come to the knowledge of it, is
" the testimony of writers who liv'd in
" that, and the following ages. And there
" is the more reason to rely upon their testi-
" mony in this case, because this is a matter
" of a simple, uncompounded nature, perfectly

* Page 326, 327.

"fectly within their knowledge; not stand‑
" ing in need of any curious niceness of
" learning, or reasoning, but level to all
" capacities; a matter in which they
" might very easily have been contradicted,
" had they represented it falsly; and a mat‑
" ter in which they could not in the first
" ages be biass'd by Interest. And here—
" I think I may say, that we have as univer‑
" sal and as unanimous a testimony of all
" writers, and historians from the apostles
" days, as could reasonably be expected,
" or desired: Every one who speaks of the
" government of the church in any place,
" witnessing that episcopacy was the settled
" form; and every one who hath occasion
" to speak of the original of it, tracing it
" up to the apostles days, and fixing it up‑
" on their decree; and what is very remar‑
" kable, no one contradicting this, either
" of the friends or enemies to christianity,
" either of the orthodox, or heretical, thro'
" those ages, in which only such assertions
" concerning this matter of fact could well
" be disprov'd."—" Were there only testi‑
" monies to be produc'd, that this was the
" government of the church in all ages, it
" would be but reasonable to conclude it
" of apostolical institution; it being so
" highly improbable that so material a
" point should be established without their
                                    " advice

" advice or decree, when we find the chur-
" ches confulting them upon every occa-
" fion, and upon matters not of greater
" importance than this. But when we find
" the fame perfons witneffing not only
" that the government of the church was
" epifcopal, but that it was of apoftolical
" inftitution, and delivered down from the
" beginning as fuch, this adds weight to
" the matter, and makes it more undoubt-
" ed. So that here are two points to
" which they bear witnefs, that this was
" the government of the church in their
" days, and that it was of apoftolical infti-
" tution. And in thefe there is fuch a con-
" ftancy, and unanimity, that even St. Je-
" rome himfelf ( who was born near 250
" years after the apoftles, and is the chief
" perfon in all that time whom the prefby-
" terians cite for any purpofe of their's )
" traces up epifcopacy to the very apoftles,
" and makes it of their inftitution ; and in
" the very place where he moft exalts pref-
" byters, he excepts ordination as a work
" always peculiar to bifhops."— He fays,
a little further on ‡, — " The teftimony
" we fpeak of, is not concerning the apof-
" tolical inftitution of the exorbitant power
" claimed by later bifhops, or of any ex-
" ternal enfigns of worldly grandeur, or
" riches appropriated to them : But meerly
" of

‡ Page 338.

"of the inftitution of one perfon to ordain and govern prefbyters, within fuch or fuch a diftrict, and according to the defign and rules of chriftianity."—He adds, †"All churches and chriftians, as far as we know, feem to have been agreed in this point, amidft all their other differences, as univerfally as can well be imagined."

Had I met with this reprefentation of ancient teftimony in a declamatory fecond-hand writer, who knew little himfelf, and only retailed, in a flourifhing manner, what he had heard from this and the other party-zealot, it would not have been furprifing; but it really was fo, to find a truly great and defervedly renowned author bringing in the ancient fathers, univerfally, unanimoufly, and conftantly affirming it to be fact, and this in all ages from the apoftles, that "the government of the church was epifcopal," and "of apoftolical inftitution;" yea, and that it was "of apoftolical inftitution too, that one perfon fhould ordain and govern prefbyters within a certain diftrict." One would imagine, from this reprefentation, that, if the writings of the fathers were confulted, epifcopacy, both the thing, and the divine inftitution of it, would fo glaringly appear to have been

acknow-

† Page 339.

acknowledged by all the fathers, in all ages from the beginning, that there would be no room left for the least debate upon the matter.

And is this the truth of fact? We shall soon see whether it is, or no. In order whereto let it be observed.

A DISTINCTION ought always to be made between the two first centuries, and the succeeding ones; for the difference between the writers in these centuries, as witnesses in the present cause, is both obviously and certainly very great. Perhaps, due attention has not been given to this distinction by the disputants on either side of the question in debate. Sir Peter King's "account of the primitive church," is, it may be, as impartial an one as any extant; but it would, as I apprehend, have been less faulty, and more perfect, if he had kept in his eye this distinction thro' the whole of his work. Nor have any of the writers on our side of the dispute, so far as I have had opportunity to read them, managed the cause with the advantage they might have done, if they had particularly pointed out the difference between the two first and following centuries, and made the use of it they might have done to their purpose. IT

It is readily acknowledged, the name bifhop, towards the clofe of the fecond century began to be an appropriated term; fignifying fomething more than the word prefbyter. In the third century, and onwards, the appropriation was common. Bifhop and prefbyter pointed out officers in the church diftinct from each other; tho' to fay precifely what, and how great, this diftinction was, will, I believe, be found to be exceeding difficult. It was undoubtedly fmall at firft. The bifhop was no more than "primus inter pares," the "head-prefbyter," the "præfes" of the confiftory. And it was by gradual fteps that he attained to that dignity and power with which he was afterwards vefted. Thofe ecclefiaftical fuperiorities and inferiorities which have, for a long time, been vifible in the chriftian world, were unknown in the firft and pureft ages. Nor did they at once take place. It was the work of time. From prime-prefbyters arofe city-bifhops; from city-bifhops, diocefan ones; from diocefan bifhops, metropolitans; from metropolitans, patriarchs; and finally, at the top of all, his holinefs the pope, claiming the character of univerfal head of the church. But to return to the diftinction between bifhops and presbyters in the centuries immediately following the fecond. And it is own'd, own'd, there was a diftinction between them; but, at the fame time, utterly denied, that the fathers are univerfal, and unanimous, in affirming it for fact, that it was a diftinction importing a fuperiority of order, or that it was of apoftolical inftitution. The learned profeffor Jamefon, in his Cyprianus Ifotimus, is pofitive in declaring,\* that even " Cyprian did not believe the divine right of epifcopacy ; " and that " he, with his colleagues, moft clearly depofe, that bifhop and presbyter, are, by Chrift's inftitution, reciprocally one and the fame." More full to our purpofe is what I find related, in Calamy's defence of nonconformity,‡ from the renowned Dr. Raynolds. The account is, " Dr. Bancroft, afterwards Arch-bifhop of Canterbury, preaching at Paul's crofs, told his auditory, that Aerius was condemned of herefy, with the confent of the univerfal church, for afferting that there was no difference, by divine right, between a bifhop and a prefbyter; and that the puritans were condemned, by the church, in Aerius. The famous Sir Francis Knolls, being furprifed at fuch doctrine, to which they were not in that day, fo much ufed as we have been fince, wrote to the learned Dr. John Raynolds, who was univerfally reckoned the wonder of his age, to defire his fenfe about the

\* Chap. 14.  ‡ Page 87, 88.

the matter. The Doctor wrote him word in anſwer, that even Bellarmine the Jeſuit owned the weakneſs of the anſwer of Epiphanius to the argument of Aerius; that Auſtin eſteemed the aſſertion of Aerius heretical, meerly becauſe he found it ſo repreſented by Epiphanius; and that Auſtin himſelf owned, that there was no difference between a biſhop and a presbyter by divine right. He cites alſo biſhop Jewel, who, when Harding had aſſerted the ſame thing as Dr. Bancroft, alledged againſt him Chryſoſtom, Auſtin, Jerom, and Ambroſe. He mentions, from Medina, ſeveral other ancient fathers; and further adds himſelf, Oecumenius, Anſelm arch-biſhop of Canterbury, another Anſelm, Gregory, and Gratian." And biſhop Stillingfleet, who appears to have been as well read in the fathers as any man in his day, or ſince, freely ſays, * " I believe, upon the ſtricteſt enquiry, Medina's judgment will prove true, that Jerom, Auſtin, Ambroſe, Sedulius, Primaſius, Chryſoſtom, Theodoret, Theophylact, were all of Aerius's judgment, as to the identity of both name and order of biſhops and presbyters in the primitive church." And again, a little onwards, † " I do as yet deſpair of finding any one ſingle teſtimony in all antiquity, which doth in plain terms aſſert epiſcopacy, as it was

* Iren. page 276. † Page 31.

was settled by the practice of the primitive church, in the ages following the apostles, to be of unalterable divine right." If any regard is to be paid to the judgment of these celebrated writers, who had made it their business to study the fathers, one would think there was reason, at least, to suspect, whether the evidence in favor of episcopacy, as an apostolical institution, is so universal and constant as has been affirmed.

But, leaving these later centuries, let us go back to the two first. And we may, with the more pertinency, do this, as the famous bishop, whose plea we are considering, has said, ‡ " We do not argue meerly
" from the testimony of so late writers as
" these (meaning Jerom and Austin) that
" episcopacy is of apostolical institution.
" We grant it doth not follow, St. Jerom
" thought so, therefore it is so. But wri-
" ters of all ages in the church witness, that
" this was the government in their days;
" that it was instituted by the apostles, and
" delivered down as such. All that we
" produce St. Jerom for in this case, is that
" it was in his time, and that he believed
" it to be apostolical, and received it as
" such: But without the testimony of the
" ages before him, I should not esteem this a
" sufficient argument that it was really so."

‡ Page 349.

And do the fathers, in the two first ages, witness what they are thus peremptorily said to do? I was at the pains, in my younger years, to read these fathers, particularly with a view to this controversy, and am obliged to say, upon my own knowledge of the matter, that the above representation is really a mistake, and a very great one too; which I candidly attribute to inattention, or some undiscerned prejudice of mind. Would the time permit, I could give you the whole of what is said, relative to the plea before us, by Barnabas, Hermas, Polycarp, Clement of Rome, Justin Martyr, Irenæus, and Clement of Alexandria, all writers in the two first centuries, and satisfy you from the very words of these fathers themselves, that they give no such evidence as is here pretended. But it must suffice to say at present,

THAT, Ignatius only excepted, the fathers, within the two first centuries, unitedly concur in speaking of bishops and presbyters much in the same language with the sacred scriptures. They never once say, either in so many words, or in words from whence it can fairly be collected, that bishops were an order in the church superior to that of presbyters; they never once say, that ordination was the work of bishops in
distinction

distinction from presbyters; they never once say, that episcopacy was the government in the church, or that it was instituted either by Christ himself, or any of his apostles; nor do they ever say, that it was so handed down to them from the beginning. Far from this, unless it strangely slipt my observation, which I do not in the least suspect it did, Clement of Alexandria, who flourished towards the close of the second century, is the first father (Ignatius excepted) who used that mode of speech, " bishops, presbyters and deacons." And the terms seem not even then to have lost their promiscuous use; for this same Clement, speaking of one under the name of a bishop, calls him, in the same sentence, the presbyter.* Irenæus, 'tis true, a few years before, once uses that form of expression, " bishops and presbyters." His words are,† " Paul called together to Miletus the bishops and presbyters of Ephesus." But, as the learned Mr. Jameson very justly observes, ‡ " for his seeming here to distinguish bishops from presbyters, this scripture where they got both names, and which Irenæus then had in view, and his frequent promiscuous using of these names, persuade me that he only respected the 19th and 28th verses,

* Blondelli Apol. Sect. xi. page 36.
† Lib. III. cap. xiv.
‡ " Nazian. querela, " sect. vi. page 157.

verses, and so took bishop and presbyter synonimically (as the apostle Paul did) for one and the same."

I MADE the remark, while upon the argument from scripture, that no instance was to be met with there of an ordination, by any person under the name of a bishop: I now add, neither have I been able to find an instance of ordination under the like name, and meaning by it a bishop as distinguished from a presbyter, in any writer till we come to the times when it is owned, a distinction obtained between these officers of the church. Episcoparians have sometimes, with an air of triumph, called for an instance of presbyterian ordination for some hundreds of years after Christ. If they will be pleased to favor us with only one example of episcopal ordination, in their sense of it, within the time above-described; which is a very considerable space; longer, counting from Christ, than from the first settlement of this country to the present day, we will take it into consideration, and give so notable a discovery all the weight it deserves. In the mean time, we hope to be excused, if we do not believe it to be a fact, either universally, or unanimously, or constantly handed down from the days of the apostles, that single persons, meaning
hereby

hereby bishops as distinguished from presbyters, exercised the ordaining power within such and such districts, or that they were ever vested with a right, by apostolical institution, so to do. We rather think, there is no just reason to affirm this to be fact, upon the testimony of any one genuine writer whatever, within the limits we are now speaking of.

THE plain truth is, no more can be collected from the writings of the fathers, till toward the close of the second century, or the coming in of the third, in favor of episcopacy, than from the scriptures themselves. And were it proper to settle the controversy by an appeal to the general suffrage of these writers, I should willingly put it on that issue; as being fully persuaded, that the advantage would lie on our side of the question, as much as if it was to be determined by the scriptures only.

IT is readily owned, the epistles ascribed to Ignatius, a truly primitive father, do as certainly, as strongly, and as constantly distinguish bishops from presbyters, as any of the writings of the third or fourth centuries. But this we esteem of little weight in the present cause, as there is so much reason to think, that these epistles are not

his

his genuine works. If he wrote thefe epiftles (which, by the way, is far from being a point beyond difpute) it is not in the leaft probable, that they came out of his hands as they now appear. The Ufferian and Voffian copies, the only ones their great advocate, bifhop Pearfon, pretends, in his ".Vindiciæ Ignatianæ," to defend, carry in them too many, and too notorious, evidences of interpolation to induce a belief, in any unprejudiced mind, that it is always the true primitive Ignatius that is the writer. For my own part, I efteem it an eafy thing to reduce it to an high degree of moral certainty, that thefe epiftles, even in their pureft editions, contain fuch unqueftionable marks of a later date than the times of Ignatius, that they ought never to be mentioned in this, or any other controverfy, unlefs to prove that religious cheat and knavery were in practice fo far back as the days of the fathers. Inftead of going into the proof of what I have now faid, which would put me upon trying your patience beyond all reafonable bounds, I fhall refer you to the two celebrated French minifters, Daille and L'arrogue, on our fide of the queftion, and the celebrated bifhops, Beveredge and Pearfon on the other; in whofe writings you will find antiquity ranfack'd, and every thing faid upon the matter

ter, that learning or good fenfe can fuggeft. Read them carefully (they are to be found in the College-library) and judge for yourfelves.

I TRUST, I may now fay, it has been made fufficiently clear, from the pofitive evidence that has been exhibited in the former part of this difcourfe, and from its not being invalidated, but rather ftrengthened, by the counter-evidence we have examined in the latter part, that the power of ordination was not depofited in the hands of bifhops as diftinguifhed from prefbyters; but that bifhops or prefbyters, meaning by thefe terms one and the fame order of officers, were vefted with power to ordain in the church of Chrift; and confequently that ordination by a council of prefbyters, as practifed by thefe churches, is valid to all the ends of the gofpel-miniftry.

THE inftitution of a lecture, on purpofe to vindicate the New-England churches in this method of ordination, may, perhaps, be reprefented to their difadvantage. Occafion may be taken herefrom to infinuate, that the method is novel and peculiar, not practifed or approbated by the other reformed proteftant churches, any more than by the church of England.

IN order to guard against suggestions of this kind, it it may be proper to let you know, that the protestant churches abroad, in common with our's, far from owning the jus divinum of episcopacy, assert a parity between bishops and presbyters, allowing the latter, equally with the former, to perform the work of ordination.

THE churches of this denomination, in Germany, speak fully to the point in their book, entitled, "Liber concordiæ," printed at Leipsic in the year 1580, and again in 1612, in which are contained "the confession of Augsburg, and the apology for it, the Smalcaldic articles, and Luther's greater and smaller catechisms." One of the "Smalcaldic articles" has these words; * " 'Tis manifest from the confession of all, our adversaries themselves, that this power [ in the foregoing words, the power mentioned was that of " preaching, dispensing the sacraments, absolution, and jurisdiction"] " is common to all that are set over the churches, whether they be called pastors, presbyters, or bishops. Jerom therefore plainly

* " — — — autem confessione omnium, etiam adversariorum — — nanc potestatem communem esse omnibus — — — distinctos gradus episcoporum— — — — — constitutos esse—Jure divino nullo — — — — et pastorem."— Jameson's

plainly affirms, that there is no difference between bifhop and prefbyter; but that every paftor was a bifhop.— Here Jerom teaches, that the diftinction of degrees between a bifhop, and a prefbyter or paftor, was only appointed by human authority. And the matter itfelf declares no lefs; for, on bifhop and prefbyter is laid the fame duty, and the fame injunction. And only ordination, in AFTER TIMES, made the difference between bifhop and paftor.—By divine right there is no difference between bifhop and paftor." Mr. Boyfe mentions the following words as further contained in this article, ‡ " Since bifhops and paftors are not different degrees by divine right, 'tis manifeft, that ORDINATION, performed by a paftor in his own church, is VALID." It is remarkable, the articles compofed at Smalcald, of which the foregoing is one, were fubfcribed by three electors, the prince Palatine, and the electors of Saxony and Brandenburg; by forty-five dukes, marqueffes, counts, and barons; by the confuls and fenators of thirty-five cities; by Luther, Melancton, Bucer, Fagius, and many other noted divines. The number of minifters, who figned thefe articles, as it has been computed, was eight thoufand.†

‡ BOYSE's clear account of the ancient epifcopacy, pag. 282.
† CALAMY's "defence of moderate non-conformity," pag. 90.

The other protestant churches as plainly assert the equality of all pastors, in point of divine right; as appears from their " public confessions of faith," which are, without all doubt, a truer and more authentic standard of their doctrine, than the private sentiments of this or the other particular person, however noted or learned. In the " confession of the churches of Helvetia," it is expresly said, * ONE and that EQUAL POWER and office is given to all ministers in the church. Certainly from the beginning, bishops or presbyters governed the church with a common care. None set himself above another, or usurped a larger power or dominion over his fellow-bishops.—Nevertheless, for order's sake, one or other of the ministers called the assembly together, proposed matters to be consulted on in the meeting, gathered the opinions of the rest, and finally took care, as much as in him lay, to prevent confusion. So St. Peter is said to have done in the acts of

the

---

* " DATA est autem omnibus in ecclesia ministris una et æqualis potestas, sive functio. Certè ab initio, episcopi vel presbyteri ecclesiam communi opere gubernaverunt. Nullus alteri se prætulit, aut sibi ampliorem potestatem dominium è in co-episcopos usurpavit. — Interea propter ordinem servandum, unus aut certus aliquis ministrorum cœtum convocavit, et in cœtu res consultandas proposuit, sententias item aliorum collegit, denique ne qua oriretur confusio, pro virili cavit. Sic legitur fecisse, in actis apostolorum, S. Petrus, qui tamen ideo nec aliis fuit præpositus, nec potestate majore cæteris præditus—". " Syntagma confessionum," page 40.

the apostles, who notwithstanding WAS NOT SET OVER THE REST, NOR VESTED WITH GREATER POWER." This confession is the more worthy of notice, as it contains virtually the sense of most of the protestant churches, besides those we have already mentioned; for it was subscribed, not only by the church of Helvetia, but by the churches of Scotland, Poland, Hungary, Geneva, Neocome, Myllhusium, &c. as is expresly declared in the preface that introduces it.

CONSONANT hereto is the confession of the French church, presented to Charles the ninth. Their thirtieth article runs thus, " We believe, that all true pastors, wherever they are placed, are endued with EQUAL POWER under that only head, the chief and sole universal bishop: And therefore no church ought to claim an empire or domination over any other church." *

THE Belgic confession is much the same. Their thirty-first article says, — " As concerning the ministers of the word of God,

---

\* " CREDIMUS omnes veros pastores, ubicunque locorum collocati fuerint, eadem et æquali inter se potestate esse præditos sub unico illo capite, summoque et solo universi episcopo Jesu Christo : Ac proinde nulli ecclesiæ licere sibi in alium imperium aut dominationem vendicare. "
Syntag. confes. pag. 84.

in whatever place they are, they have all the SAME POWER AND AUTHORITY, as being all the ministers of Christ, that only universal bishop and head of the church."†

To these may be added the Waldenses and Albigenses, of whom Alphonsus de Castro relates, " that they denied any difference between bishop and presbyter, and herein differed nothing from Aerius ; " which also may be learnt from Thuan, who compares them with " the English nonconformists." The Waldenses were in this, as in the rest of their articles, followed by J. Huss, and his adherents, who also asserted, " there ought to be no difference between bishops and presbyters, or among priests." Yea, so universal hath this doctrine, of the identity of bishop and presbyter, been, that it hath, all along, by the Romanists, been reckoned a prime doctrine of Rome's opposers. ‡

'Tis readily acknowledged, in most of the protestant churches there are ecclesiastical officers, who bear the style of bishops, super-intendants, inspectors, or seniors ; as may

---

† " QUANTUM vero attinet divini verbi ministros, ubicunque locorum sint, eandem illi potestatem et authoritatem habent, ut qui omnes sint Christi, unici illius episcopi universalis, unicique capitis ecclesiæ"—. Syntag. confes. pag. 142.

‡ Jameson's Nazian. querela, pag. 96.

may be seen in Stillingfleet's "Irenicum," where these churches are all mentioned by name: But, as that learned author observes, "all these reformed churches acknowledge no such thing as a divine right of episcopacy, but stifly maintain Jerom's opinion of the primitive equality of gospel-ministers."\*. Nor could they consistently do any other; for they have, at bottom, no other than presbyterian ordination among them. "Luther, Calvin, Bucer, Melancton, Bugenhagius," &c. and all the first reformers and founders of these churches, who ordained ministers among them, were themselves presbyters, and no other. And tho', in some of these churches, there are ministers which are called super-intendants, or bishops; yet these are only "primi inter pares," the first among equals; not pretending to any superiority of order. Having themselves no other orders than what either presbyters gave them, as were given them as presbyters, they can convey no other to those they ordain. †

Our

\* Iren. page 411.
† "THE diffenting gentleman's answer to White," page 45. At the bottom of this page, 'tis added, "The Danish church is, at this time, governed by bishops. But they look upon episcopacy as only an human institution; and the first proteftant prelates in that kingdom were ordained by Burgenhagius, [he ordained no less than seven of them at one time] a meer presbyter; who, by consequence, could convey no other than a presbyterian ordination to their successors ever since."

Our adversaries indeed do themselves, when they speak out their mind, freely tell us, that " all the transf-marine reformed churches are really presbyterian." Dr. Heylin, upon this account, thro' a large folio, bespatters, with the blackest of railings and calumnies, every one of the reformed churches in particular. Howel also makes Calvin " the first broacher of the presbyterian religion." And says, " Geneva lake swallowed up the episcopal see ; and church lands were made secular, which was the white they levelled at. This Geneva bird flew thence to France, and hatched the Huguenots, which make about a tenth part of that people. It took wing also to Bohemia and Germany, high and low, as the Palatinate, the land of Hesse, and the confederate provinces of the States of Holland."†

If, to the protestant churches that have been mentioned, we add the congregational dissenting brethren in England, who, at the revolution, are supposed to have made nearly two thousand churches ; the large body of presbyterian dissenters in the north of Ireland ; as also the dissenters of other denominations in Britain, the united provinces, and other parts of Europe, who are all of one mind as to the right of presbyters to ordain : — I say, if we add all these together,

† Jameson's Nazian. querela, pag. 95.

gether, they will make a number vaſtly greater than that which conſtitutes the epiſcopal church of England, ſhould we take into the computation every member of this church. But ſhould we leave out of the reckoning thoſe, who live in love and harmony with diſſenters, eſteeming their ordinations valid, tho' not according to the eſtabliſhed form, and bring ſuch only into the account, who are ſo ſtrenuous for the jus divinum of epiſcopacy as to nullify all ordinations, unleſs by a biſhop, in their ſenſe of the word, they will ſink into a number too inconſiderable to be mentioned in compariſon with the many, who differ from them in their ſentiments. Not that we rely upon numbers. The ſcriptures only can determine, what is truth in the preſent debate. But ſtill, it is a ſatisfaction to us, that our ordinations are ſuch as agree with the declared ſentiments of almoſt the whole proteſtant world. And our ſatisfaction is the greater, as we have ſo much reaſon to believe, that they agree with the principles even of the church of England itſelf, at the beginning of the reformation, and for ſome time afterwards.

THE generality of it's pious and learned divines in thoſe days, whether of higher or lower dignity, were far from inſiſting on

on the divine right of epifcopacy; as may be feen in quotations, from their writings to this purpofe, by the celebrated Stillingfleet. * And it is worthy of of fpecial notice here, in Henry the eighth's time, when things were tending to a reformation, the arch-bifhops, bifhops, archdeacons, and clergy of England, in their book intitled, " the inftruction of a chriftian man," fubfcribed with all their hands and dedicated to the king an. 1537; and king Henry himfelf, in his book ftiled, " a neceffary erudition for any chriftian man," approved by both houfes of parliament, prefaced with his own epiftle, and publifhed by his command, exprefsly refolve, " that priefts and bifhops by God's law are one and the fame, and that the power of ordination and excommunication belongs equally to them both." † Herewith, it may be further noted, agrees the manufcript mentioned by bifhop Stillingfleet, in which archbifhop Cranmer, one of the affembly, called together by the fpecial command of king Edward fixth, in anfwer to his queftions, has thefe words, ‡ " bifhops and priefts were at one time, and were not two things, but one office in the beginning of Chrift's religion." The bifhop of Afaph, Therleby, Redman, and Cox were all of
and

* Irenicum, pag. 394, and onwards.
† Calamy's " defence of moderate non-conformity," p. 90, 91.
‡ Irenicum, page 392.

the same opinion with the arch-bishop; and the two latter expresly cite the opinion of Jerom with approbation. Upon which the learned writer, to whom we are indebted for this account observes,* "Thus we see by the testimony chiefly of him, who was instrumental in our reformation, that he owned not episcopacy, as a distinct order from presbytery, of divine right, but only a prudential constitution of the civil magistrate for the better governing in the church." This same arch-bishop Cranmer was "the first of six and forty, who, in the time of king Henry the eighth, affirmed (in a book called "the bishop's book," to be seen in "Fox's martyrology") that "the difference of bishops and presbyters was a device of the ancient fathers, and not mentioned in the scripture." ‡

IT is indeed beyond dispute, that the episcopal form of government was settled, at the reformation, upon a very different foot from that of a jus divinum. How else can it be accounted for, that not only in king Henry the eighth's reign, but likewise in king Edward the sixth's, the bishops took out commissions from the crown, by which they were to hold their bishopricks only during the king's pleasure, and were impowered

---

* Stillingfleet, in his Irenicum, page 393.
‡ J. Owen's "plea for scripture-ordination," page 114.

powered in the king's name, as his delagates, to perform all the parts of the episcopal function ? Archbishop Cranmer, that excellent and holy martyr, set an example to the rest in taking out one of them. \* This method of acting is certainly better adjusted to a constitution, founded on policy, than divine right. Nay, as far from the beginning of the reformation as the days of queen Elisabeth, in the articles of religion agreed upon, the English form of church-government was only determined " to be agreeable to God's word ; " which † had been a very low and diminishing expression, had they looked on it as absolutely prescribed in scripture, as the only necessary form to be observed in the church.

The truth is, says Mr. Owen, this notion of the jus divinum of episcopacy, as a superior order, was first promoted in the church of England by arch-bishop Laud. Dr. Holland, the king's professor of divinity in Oxon, was much offended with him, for asserting it in a disputation for his degrees. He checked him publicly, and told him, " he went about to make a division between the English, and the other reformed churches." ‡

AND

---

\* Burnet's abridg. of the hist. of the reform. Vol. II. p. 7.
† Irenicum, page 393, 394.
‡ " Plea for scripture-ordination, " page 115.

AND it was in this archbishop's time, that the point of re-ordination began to be urged. Through his influence, as Mr. Prin tells us, \* bishop Hall re-ordained Mr. John Dury, a minister of the reformed church. But the old church of England did not require or practise re-ordination. In king Edward the sixth's time, PeterMartyr, Martin Bucer, and P. Fagius had ecclesiastical preferments in the church of England without re-ordination.† Mr. WilliamWhitingham was made dean of Durham, about 1563 ; tho' ordained by presbyters only. ‡ In like manner, Mr. Travers, ordained by a presbyter beyond sea, was seven years lecturer at the temple, and had the bishop of London's letter for it. § And even in the reign of king James the first, the validity of ordination by presbyters was not set aside ; as appears from the case of the three presbyters that were consecrated bishops for Scotland at London. Before their consecration, Dr. Andrews, bishop of Ely, moved the question, " whether they should not be first episcopally ordained presbyters, that they might be capable of being admitted into the order of bishops ? " Upon which arch-bishop Bancroft ( a most rigid assertor of episcopacy ) answered, " there was

---

\* " Plea for scripture-ordination, " page 117.
† Ibid page 118. ‡ Ibid page 121. § Ibid page 122.

was no need of it, since ordination by presbyters was valid." The bishop of Ely yeilded; and without repeating their ordination as presbyters, they were consecrated bishops.\*

How far this practice, in the episcopal church, at home, in those days, would be countenanced at present, I don't pretend to determine; but thus much has been said by your highly esteemed divinity-professor, upon a proper occasion; whose words are well worth transcribing here, " I cannot
" learn, whether there has been even in
" England, to this very day, properly any
" public and express assertion of the " divine right " of prelacy, either by parlia-
" ment, or convocation. I think no such
" thing can be found in the thirty-nine ar-
" ticles, or in the homilies, or in the form
" of ordination, or in the common prayer-
" book, &c. Unless it may be thought con-
" tained in the preface to the book of ordi-
" nation, where there is a hint that seems
" to carry such an aspect; but, I believe,
" will appear too slender a foundation to
" build upon, in the present case; especial-
" ly if we remember who were the chief
" compilers of that book; and what rea-
" son we have to conclude, they were of
" the judgment, that " priests and bishops
" are,

\* Pierce's vindication, part I. page 167.

" are, by God's law, one and the same";
" and that the episcopal dignity is rather
" by custom, than by divine institution." *

WHAT has been offered will, I believe, be tho't sufficent to make it evident, that ordination by presbyters is no new thing under the sun, a singularity peculiar to the New-England churches; since we have seen it approved by so many of the protestant reformed churches, and by the church of England itself, at least in its first protestant and reformed state, and for a considerable time afterwards. And had there been an establishment, in those days, putting the power of ordination into the hands of presbyters, it would have been, according to the then general opinion, as agreeable to scripture, as that which put it into the hands of bishops. Possibly, the latter would not have been the establishment, had it not been for ecclesiastical dignities and revenues; which enter not into the jus divinum of the thing.

I SHALL now put an end to the trial of your patience, by speaking a few words to the young gentlemen of the college, who are under tuition in order to their being formed for usefulness, when they go out into the world.

WE

* " Sober remarks," page 11.

We have such a question as that in the prophesies of the prophet Jeremiah, "Hath a nation changed their gods, which yet are no gods?" And it beautifully represents the strength of a people's attachment to the religious sentiments and practices of their fore-fathers, the difficulty with which they are wrought upon to depart from them. Even the nations, who have been taught by their ancestors, to worship idol-gods, which, in reality, are no gods, will not easily change the object of their devotion. 'Tis not, it is owned, a sufficient plea in favor of any religious principles, or mode of worship, that they are such as were handed down to us from our fathers. They may, notwithstanding, be superstitious, absurd, and sinful. And should this be the case, filial reverence towards the father of our spirits should take place of the reverence due to the fathers of our flesh. But should they, on the other hand, be consonant to the dictates of uncorrupted reason, and the truth of revelation, 'twould be strange, if posterity should desert them; especially, if, instead of adhering to them, they should go back to those their progenitors had renounced, and were really right in having so done. This, if I mistake not, is a thought well worthy of the attention of our sons, who are sent to this collegiate-school,

school to be fitted for public service. We don't advise you to hold fast the religion of your country, meerly because it is the religion of your fathers. This would be to act below your dignity as intelligent and moral agents. But still it deserves, on this account, your serious examination. And we would exhort you to the greatest care and diligence in studying the reasons upon which the religion you have been educated in is grounded ; and, in this way, we doubt not but you will, and upon the foot of just and solid conviction, be firmly attached to it. We would particularly recommend it to you thoroughly to enquire into the reasons of that " mode of worship," and " form of church order," which your progenitors left every thing that was dear to them, in their native land, that they might enjoy themselves in this place of retreat, and transmit to their posterity: Especially would we recommend this to those among you, who are designed for the ministry; and the more exact and critical you are in your enquiries upon this head, the less will be our concern as to the event ; being fully satisfied, you will find abundant reason, with all freedom, to join in communion with the New-England churches, and to settle in them as pastors, in the method of investiture common among us, should you be called thereto in the providence of God.

WE advise you all, our beloved sons, to make the wisest and best use of the rich advantages you are here favoured with, to lay the foundation for such acquirements in learning as will make you eminent blessings to the world, in the various stations of life, when you go from hence. 'Tis pity any of you should misimprove the valuable price that is put into your hands; a thousand pities you should idle away your time, much more that you should misspend it in needless diversion, in vain company, or, what is vastly worse, in the pursuit of those follies, by which young men are too apt to be drawn aside and enticed.

ABOVE all, we advise and beseech you to cultivate in your minds a serious sense of the things pertaining to the kingdom of God and Christ. Rest not satisfied with any attainments, till you have secured the justification of life, the sanctification of the spirit, and the adoption of children. You may then live joyfully, and you will die safely. The great God will be the guide of your youth, your guide thro' the world, your guide thro' death, and your portion for ever. AMEN.

APPENDIX.

# APPENDIX,

Giving a brief historical account of the epistles ascribed to Ignatius; and exhibiting some of the many reasons, why they ought not to be depended on as his uncorrupted works.

IF we form our judgment of Ignatius from the accounts that are given of him by some modern authors, we must conceive of him as FIRST among the oriental worthies, not only in ecclesiastical dignity, but in piety, learning, and every other endowment, whether natural or spiritual. And, possibly, such sentiments concerning him may be just; tho' there is no way in which, at present, we can know them to be so. The fathers, who lived in the two or three first centuries, say but little about him. They don't so much as tell us, where he was born, how educated, when brought over to the christian faith, or by the instrumentality of what persons or means. They have indeed left nothing upon record, save the manner of his going out of the world, from whence his character, as distinguished from that of others of the same age, can be particularly drawn.

He is spoken of, in after-times, as bishop of Antioch.* But it would lead us into wrong tho'ts of this stile, should we take our idea of it from that superiority to which bishops were then exalted. 'Tis probable, the fathers, who call him bishop, esteemed him such in the sense the word was understood in their day; but as the sense of this word was different then from what it was in the age in which Ignatius flourished, they might take more into it's meaning, than it at first intended. Prime-pastor, head-presbyter, is the most that was meant by his being bishop of Antioch, at the time when he sustained this relation to that church.

If there is no room to question his dying a martyr, the manner and circumstances of the fact, as they are related in " the acts of his martyrdom, " may reasonably be disputed. The story of Trajan's sending him to Rome, after his condemnation at Antioch, that he " might be thrown to wild beasts, " does not seem, however defended with his epistles, to be any of the most probable. " For wherefore should Ignatius of all others be brought to Rome to suffer, when the " Proconsuls," and the " Præsides provinciarum, " did every where, in time of persecution, execute their power in punishing christians at their own tribunals, without sending them

to

---

\* ORIGEN; a writer in the third century, is the first that mentions him under this character. He is herein followed by the succeeding fathers: Tho' they differ in the place they give him in the line of succession; some putting Euodius before him, and others Ignatius next to the apostle Peter, or Paul, or both. This makes a difficulty not unlike to that of Clement's succession in the see of Rome. The episcoparians take different methods to solve it; which it is not my business, at present, to examine.

so long a journey to Rome, to be martyr'd there. And how came Ignatius to make so many, and such strange, excursions as he did, by the story, if the soldiers that were his guard were so cruel to him, as he complains they were." *

But however it might be as to circumstances, the thing itself, his dying for the sake of Christ, is not denied; tho' the year of his martyrdom cannot be certainly fix'd. Basnage ranks it among the obscurities of chronology.† Bishop Pearson, bishop Loyd, Pagi, LeClerc and Fabricius place it A. D. 115 or 116. But Du Pin, Tillemont, and Dr. Cave, in the 10th of Trajan, 107. Perhaps, this last period is by far the more probable.

As to the epistles that have been ascribed to this primitive father, and given rise to so much dispute in the protestant world, the most perfect account of them, I have been able to collect, is briefly this.

The first edition of them came out in the year 1494 or 5; containing only three latin epistles, one to "the Virgin Mary," the other two to "St. John." A. D. 1497 or 8, Faber Stapulensis published eleven more latin epistles, which were several times reprinted at Stratsburg, and once at Basil. Champerius afterwards impressed the above three and eleven epistles, with the addition of another " ad Mariam Cassabolitam." This was done at Cologn in 1536, and made in all fifteen epistles. They were as yet extant only in latin, and thus they remained, in still repeated impressions, till 1557, when Pacæus printed them in greek, with the latin translation of Perionius. The following year Gesner published

* " Iren." pag. 298. † Annal. 107. § vi.

published them in greek likewife, with the verfion of Brunnerus. This Gefner affumed the honor of being the firft, who had made thefe epiftles public in greek. But Pacæus is allowed, both by DuPin, and bifhop Pearfon, to have been the firft editor of them in this language. [ N. B. Thefe greek editions contain only twelve of the fifteen epiftles. ] In the year 1608, the edition of Meftræus came forth; and finally that of Vedelius in 1623, with large commentaries.

This was the ftate of the " Ignatian epiftles, " when arch-bifhop Ufher firft faw them. Upon reading them, he took notice, that three ancient Englifh divines * had formerly quoted a paffage from them in the very fame words, in which it had been quoted by Theodoret, which words were not to be found in the prefent editions, either greek or latin; and from hence he concluded, there muft be fome manufcript-copy of thefe epiftles in England. He made diligent fearch, and at length found two copies, one at Cambridge in the library of Caius college, the other in the private library of bifhop Montague; containing an ancient verfion different from the vulgar. He compared it with the paffages cited by the fathers, and, finding a good agreement between them, tho't fit to put out an edition of " the Ignatian epiftles, " from this verfion; which was printed in 1644. Not long after this, the learned Voffius found, in the duke of Tufcany's library at Florence, a greek manufcript, containing fix of thefe epiftles, fuppofed to be the fame that are mentioned by Eufebius and Jerom; which,

agreeing

* Wodeford, Robert Lincolnienfis, and Tiffington.
" Hammond's anfw. to animadver. on his defence," pag. 50

# APPENDIX.

agreeing with arch-bishop Usher's copies, he published at Amsterdam in 1646, with the addition of a seventh, that to " the Romans, " much amended from the latin version. This last epistle, in 1684, was published at Paris, by Mr. Ruinart, from a supposed uninterpolated copy.

From this account of the epistles that go under the name of Ignatius, 'tis obvious to divide them into three classes.

The first contains those three that are extant only in latin, inscribed to " the Virgin Mary, " and " St. John." But they are of so little importance, that learned men scarce think it worth while to be at the pains to prove them spurious.

The second comprehends the epistles that are printed in greek, but not mentioned by Eusebius, or Jerom. And these are five in number. The first, to " Mary Cassabolita ; " the second, to " the inhabitants of Tarsus ; " the third, to " the Antiochians ; " the fourth, to " Hero the deacon of Antioch ; " the fifth, to " the Phillippians. " Bellarmine, Baronius, Passevin, and a few others, give credit to these epistles as the real works of Ignatius ; but they are herein opposed by almost the whole body, especially, of protestant writers, who look upon them to be evidently suppositious.

In the third class are comprised the seven epistles, which are supposed to be mentioned by Eusebius and Jerom ; which are as follow. The first, to " the Ephesians ; the second, to " the Magnesians ; " the third, to " the Trallians ; " the fourth, to
" the

"the Romans;" the fifth, to "the Philadelphians"; the sixth, to "theSmyrnæans"; the seventh, "to Polycarp." It may be observed here, archbishop Usher, and others after him, reject this last; looking upon the six former as the only ones commemorated by Eusebius: Tho' there are those, on the contrary, who, perhaps not with so much reason, conclude he takes notice of the whole seven.

As for the seven greek epistles, in this last class, they may be considered as extant in the editions of them before, or since, the days of Usher and Vossius.

IN the former consideration of them, they are stiled "the larger epistles," and generally discarded as unworthy of so primitive a father as Ignatius. Calvin, the Century-writers, Whittaker, Parker, Scultet, Rivet, and others, always declared this to be their opinion of them: Tho' the advocates for prelacy, such as Whitgift, Bilson, Dounam, Heylyn, Taylor, and others, professed a belief of them as truly genuine. And as such they were, in those days, appealed to, in the cause of episcopacy, with as much zeal and frequency as they have been since. But these "larger epistles" are now, I may say, universally given up as incapable of defence. The learned bishop Pearson freely owns, that they are corrupted and interpolated: And tho' he commends the industry of Vedelius in what he has done to distinguish between what is genuine, and interpolated, in them; yet he thinks, at the same time, that he has not sufficiently done it; and, in a word, does not undertake their defence, in these editions of them.

THESE

# APPENDIX. 97

THESE epistles, considered in the latter view, as published from the " Cantabrigian " and " Florentine " copies, are called the " shorter ones, " and represented by the episcoparians to be the uncorrupted works of Ignatius; and, as such, we are turned to them, upon all occasions, as containing full evidence of the superiority of bishops to presbyters in order and power.

UPON which, I can't but put you upon minding the conduct of, at least, some of our opponents. The " larger epistles " of Ignatius they once earnestly contended for against all that opposed them, and constantly repaired to them as the great support of their cause. But now they are willing to throw them by as useless; the " shorter editions " of Usher and Vossius being the only ones to be depended on. They could not be prevailed with, by any methods of reasoning, to give up Ignatius in the " former editions, " till they had got others, from other copies, to supply their place. And now they readily see the force of the arguments, they before esteemed as nothing better than meer cavils. It certainly looks as tho' they imagined their cause stood in absolute need of Ignatius, and were willing to part with him in " former editions, " only because they have others to substitute in their room, that they can better manage: Nor can one well forbear thinking, if " other editions, " from still other manuscripts, should come forth, more defensible than these they now have, they would as readily quit " these, " and cry up " them. ".

BUT however uncorrupt the " shorter Ignatian epistles " are said to be, there are some, and of

M the

the first rank too for learning, who have openly declared their opinion of them as spurious; and a still greater number look upon them as interpolated, and to a degree that renders them unfit to be repaired to, in order to know the mind of the true Ignatius.

THE strange silence of primitive antiquity concerning epistles under the name of Ignatius is given, by the learned Daille, as a good reason to suspect, that he never wrote any. There is no controversy about the fact itself, namely, that none of the writers, whose works are still remaining, mention epistles wrote by Ignatius, either a less or greater number, till we come into the fourth century, three only excepted. And 'tis really a disputable point, to say the least, whether any of these three, all circumstances considered, are to be looked upon as proper vouchers in the case.* But should they be
allowed

---

* Polycarp, Irenæus, and Origen, are the three fathers, who are said to mention epistles wrote by Ignatius. The sentence in Polycarp, which takes notice of these epistles, is that which concludes his own epistle. 'Tis an independant paragraph, and may be considered, either as an original part of the epistle, or an after-addition, without the least damage to its connection or sense. In this view of it, Daille and L'arroque look upon it as an interpolation; and for this reason, because it speaks of Ignatius as yet alive, and not come to his last sufferings; while, in the ninth section, he is directly mentioned as dead, and gone to the Lord; which, as they argue, is an inconsistency, it would be a dishonor to charge upon Polycarp. So far as I am able to judge, neither bishop Pearson, nor arch-bishop Wake have said that which is sufficient to take off the force of this arguing. As for Irenæus, the manner of his introducing what he gives us from Ignatius is this, " quemadmodum quidam de nostris dixit, " as one from among us said; which is as properly applicable
to

allowed to be so, 'tis notwithstanding an unaccountable thing, that, for the full space of two hundred years, no more notice should be taken of the writings of this primitive father, if he left any. For let it be considered,

IGNATIUS

to a VERBAL, as WRITTEN saying: For which reason I can't but think, notwithstanding all that has been offered in favor of this testimony, that Mr. Lardner speaks the exact truth, when he says, " 'Tis disputable, whether he cites a passage of a WRITING, or only mentions some WORDS or EXPRESSIONS of Ignatius, which might be spoken by him upon the near view of his martyrdom." The testimonies from Origen (who, by the way, was a writer in the third century) are two. The first is taken from " the prologue to the commentaries on Canticles, " that goes under his name. If he was the real author, (which is tho't questionable) we have it only in the version of Ruffin, who is represented as taking a shameful liberty in all his translations of Origen, to alter, add or diminish; insomuch that there is no knowing what is his, and what is Origen's. 'Tis, I conclude, for this reason, that neither arch bishop Usher nor Dr. Hammond do make use of this Origenical testimony in the evidence they exhibit in favor of the " Ignatian epistles. " The other testimony is cited from " his homily on Luke." This also is suspected to be the work of some latin author; but if Origen really wrote it, 'tis extant only in latin: And if it was translated by Jerom, as is pretended, there is no knowing what is truly Origen's. Du Pin says, the versions of Jerom are not more exact than Ruffin's. And Ruffin complains of the liberty Jerom took in his translations, as Jerom complains, in like manner, of him. And certainly no great credit ought to be given to translations which were done with unbounded licence. I may pertinently add here, 'tis a shrewd circumstance, giving reason to suspect that Origen never mentioned the " Ignatian epistles " in his writings, that he is silently passed over by Eusebius. For no one was a greater admirer of Origen, nor was any one more particularly versed in his writings. And as he expresly refers to the above passages in Polycarp and Irenæus, 'tis strange he should take no notice of those in Origen, if they had, in his day, been contained in his writings.

IGNATIUS was a person that lived in the first age of christianity; was personally known to, and acquainted with, at least, some of the apostles, and many of those who had been conversant with them; and he was (as is generally supposed) fixed, by the apostle Peter, or Paul, or both, in the pastoral office at Antioch, a noted city in itself, and the more so on account of its being the place, where believers were first distinguished by the name of christians. These are considerations that open to us so much of the character of this ancient father, as to leave it past doubt, that he was not so obscure a person as to be unknown in those days. Besides, he was a glorious martyr for the cause of Christ; and, if he really wrote these epistles, the circumstances of his martyrdom were more signally illustrious, than ever attended any other martyrdom before, or since, that we have any record of. For he was condemned at Antioch to die at Rome; and, in order to the execution of this sentence, was conveyed by a band of soldiers, as a prisoner of Jesus Christ, through all the gospelised places, that lay between these two greatly distant cities. Such circumstances could not well fail of spreading his fame, and occasioning his being universally known, and talk'd of, among christians. A primitive father, and first-pastor of one of the most celebrated christian churches, to be carried, as it were, thro' the world, in bonds for the name of Christ; — it could not but be taken notice of, by all the churches, as he passed along: Nor is it conceivable, but that his name upon this account, should be had in remembrance. If he had been an obscure person before, these observables would have " set him on a hill, " and put him under an advantage, beyond

any

any of the fathers of the same age, of being commemorated in after-writings. Such are the circumstances under which we are to conceive of the supposed author of these epistles.

AND extraordinary ones attend the epistles themselves. For they were wrote, if at all wrote by Ignatius, in the capacity of a " prisoner of death," and while actually on his journey to be " devoured by wild beasts " : Nor were they wrote to a particular friend, upon some private concern ; nor yet to here and there an obscure church, but to as noted ones as had then been formed ; and this, if we may credit the episcoparians, upon matters of the greatest importance : Which are considerations that won't suffer us to think, that " these epistles " were either unknown to the world, or esteemed worthy of no notice. Six epistles wrote and sent to as many famous churches, by the head-pastor of Antioch, upon the most momentous affairs, and at so solemn a time as that of his being about to die for the sake of Christ, could not but have occasioned great talk in the christian world ; nor is there room to doubt, that they would have had a very distinguishing value put upon them : Nay, they must have been esteemed the most celebrated monuments of all uninspired antiquity, and as such have been universally known and regarded, especially by the learned writers in those times. And 'tis really a surprising thing, that so little respect should be paid to them for the full space of 200 years, after their compofure ; and what makes the matter still more strange is, that the writings of others of the same age are particularly named, or quoted. And why should the writings of Ignatius, the most famous of them all,

be

be treated with such unbecoming neglect?—There is certainly some reason, from these hints, to suspect, whether Ignatius was the real author of these epistles.

'Tis urged, if he did not pen them, they were forged before the days of Eusebius, that is, between the beginning of the second, and the coming in of the fourth century; which is represented as a thing altogether incredible. 'Tis readily acknowledged, this religious knavery was practised, if at all, within the time specified. And I freely own for myself still further, that I really tho't it an incredible thing, it should be practised within this period, till, by better acquaintance with antiquity, I was fully convinced I had been under a great mistake. Perhaps, the knavish forgeries, within this term, were as numerous as they have ever been since, in the same space of time. Scarce one of the apostles, or first most eminent fathers, have escaped being personated by some wretched impostor, in some piece or other, they have palmed on the world under their name. Nay, our blessed Lord himself has been thus basely used. And there is no one tolerably versed in the ancient writings, but knows this to be true. Hegesippus, (contemporary with Justin Martyr, who flourished about the year 150) discoursing of " apocryphal books," says, at least, of some of them, that they * " were made by the heretics of his time." Irenæus observes, that † " the heretics in his day had an innumerable multitude of spurious and apocryphal books, which they had forged to delude the more weak and ignorant sort of persons." Origen, Jerom, Epiphanius, Ambrose,

* Euseb. lib. IV. cap. xxii.
† Adverf. Hæref. lib. I. cap. xvii.

Ambrose, and others, tell us of great numbers of these books made use of by the heretics in their times. Of these books, some are quite lost, not so much as the names, or the least part of them, remaining. Of others, there are some few fragments in the writings of the fathers, without mentioning the books from whence they were taken. Of others, there are undoubted fragments, with the names of the books out of which they are cited. Others are still extant, at least, in part. The reader may see a surprisingly large catalogue of these forged books, in DuPin's "ecclesiastical history;" and a much larger one still in Mr. Jones's "method of settling the canon of the new-testament": From both which authors, he may meet with what will abundantly satisfy him, that they are indeed forgeries, and were imposed on the world long before the days of Eusebius.

AND not only were books forged under the name of inspired persons, but of some of the most famous primitive fathers. Such are the " Recognitions " fathered on Clement of Rome; the "Clementines," as also the " Epitome of the Clementine acts of Peter "; not to say any thing of the pretended " apostolical constitutions and canons," said to be penned by Clement. Such are Polycarp's " letter to Dionysius the Areopagite," and his " discourse on St. John's death". These are all of them evidently spurious pieces, and most of them universally owned to be so. And yet, they were forged before the fourth century. So that, be our opinion of the times before Eusebius as it will, some there were, even in those times, who were both impudent and knavish enough to be guilty of such a fraud, as that we suppose might have been practised, under the name of Ignatius: And the supposition of his being thus fraudulently dealt by is so far from being an incredible thing, that it only adds one to the many religious frauds, which were committed in those days, and under the names of much better men than he can be pretended to be.——

AFTER all, 'tis possible, I own, Ignatius might be the writer of these epistles: Nor will I pretend to determine, that he was not: Tho' I am inclined to think, most unprejudiced persons, from what has been offered, will be disposed to question, whether they are so certainly his, as to leave no reasonable room for, at least, some doubt in the case.

BUT should it be conceded, that these epistles were certainly wrote by Ignatius, we shall, notwithstanding, hope to be excused, if we lay no great weight upon what is cited from them; and for this very good reason, because we judge they are so interlarded with corrupt mixtures, as not fairly to exhibit the real sentiments of the primitive father, whose name they bear. *

WHAT

---

* IT should be remembred here 'tis not only the truth of fact, that Ignatius has been basely and fraudulently dealt with, no less than eight of the fifteen epistles that bear his name being FORGERIES, and owned to be so; but 'tis fact likewise, and acknowledged as such, that the other seven, in all the editions of them, before Usher and Vossius, have been SO CORRUPTED by some knavish interpolator, as that they ought not to be received as his genuine works. We don't argue from hence, that the " later editions " must be corrupted also; but thus much is obviously and certainly deducible herefrom, that they MAY be so; that the supposition is quite easy and natural, as falling in with what has already been practised upon these epistles.

# APPENDIX.

WHAT we have to offer in support of this judgement, takes in so many particulars, that it would require a vast deal more room than can at present be spared to consider them. I shall therefore wholly pass them over, and confine myself to one thing only, viz. what is here said concerning the officers of the churches he writes to. And I the rather pitch upon this, because the discourse upon this head so runs through all the epistles, ( one only excepted, the epistle to the " Romans " * ) bears so great a part in them, and is so mingled with almost every paragraph, that if what is offered upon this point is not worthy of the true Ignatius, or evidently exhibits the marks of an age POSTERIOR to that in which he lived, they will have fastened on them the charge of corruption, unfitting them to be depended on in the present, or indeed any other, debate.

THREE things I have here to say, which I esteem worthy of particular notice, and shall distinctly mention.

I. THERE is vastly more said upon the head of church-officers, than might be expected from the true Ignatius. The seven epistles, in the translation of arch-bishop Wake, take up about 50 pages in octavo; and the extracts I have made from them, as they relate only to bishops and presbyters, will fill at least ten; tho' they are made from but six

---

\* 'Tis observable, this epistle is the only one that is perfectly useless to the episcopal cause. For it differs from all the rest in this, that it don't once distinguish bishops from presbyters; and, if I don't misremember, the word bishop is but once used throughout the whole epistle.

of the seven epistles. Now, considering the circumstances of Ignatius, when he wrote these epistles, 'tis highly improbable, he should have his heart so much set upon the honor and power of the clergy, as, in all of them, to be so very lavish in his discourse upon this point. He was now a "prisoner of death," and on "his journey to the place of execution": And if he found within himself a disposition to write to the several churches, as he went along, 'tis really strange, he should be so large in his encomiums, exhortations, directions, cautions, and insinuations, all tending to exalt the clergy, and bespeak for them the highest reverence, and most profound subjection. Had he thus wrote in one or two only of his letters, the special circumstances of the churches to whom he wrote might, perhaps, be pleaded in his excuse: But it cannot be supposed, so many churches should be so ignorant of their own constitution, or of the duty they owed to the officers set over them; or that they had been so faulty in their behaviour towards the clergy, as to make it proper for a condemned pastor, just going out of the world, so to write to them, as if the main thing suitable to be said was, "that they had very worthy, and God-becoming bishops and presbyters, whom they ought to revere and honor as God the Father, and his son Jesus Christ." There is plainly much more spoken upon the subject of the clergy, and their rights, than upon any other, tho' of the most fundamental importance; which looks very strange. It would certainly do so in epistles, wrote at present, under like circumstances; and the rather, as the same things are not only mentioned in all the epistles, but in most of them needlessly repeated,

and

and in some of them repeated over and over again so as to be quite fulsome. Should a bishop, at this day, while in the near view of death for religion's sake, write epistles to the churches after this pattern, I scruple not to give it as my opinion, that the general thought of the world concerning him, in this day of christian liberty, would be, that over-heated zeal for clerical honor and power had put him out of the possession of himself. This leads

II. To the next consideration, namely, the "lofty descriptions" that are given, in these epistles, of the officers of the christian church, with the "exorbitant claims of power and dominion" made on their behalf. The language to this purpose is truly extraordinary, not at all consonant to the age of the true Ignatius, nor indeed worthy of so primitive a father and martyr. What other thought can we entertain of those numerous expressions, which represent bishops as " presiding in the place of God " : which compare them to " God the Father, and to Jesus Christ the son of the Father " : which declare it our duty to " receive them as the Lord, to reverence them as Jesus Christ," yea, " to follow them even as Christ does the Father " : which caution against " resisting the bishop, left we should disobey God " : which command us " so to obey the bishop, and subject ourselves to him, as to do nothing without him " : which, " without the bishop ", deem it " unlawful either to baptise, or celebrate the sacrament, or indeed do any thing, however reasonable it may appear to us " : which exhort to be " so one with the bishop, as Christ is one with the Father ; and so to do nothing without him, as Christ did nothing without the Father " :

which

which make so great account of " obedience and subjection to the bishop," that they who " do any thing without him " are esteemed " doing the devil a service "; and " those that remain with him " are, upon this account only, thought worthy of the character " of belonging to Christ "; and are represented " as walking not as men, but according to Christ ": Yea, in so high estimation is obedience to the officers of the church, with the author of these epistles, that he even " pawns his soul for those who obey the bishop, presbyters and deacons," and desires " his portion in God may be with such."

THESE, and like, expressions, so frequently to be met with in these epistles, can't easily be supposed to have been penned by the true Ignatius. In their literal strict sense, they are unworthy of any pious writer; much more of the celebrated father, to whom they are ascribed: Nor can it be denied, that they aggrandise bishops beyond all reasonable bounds, and plead for the most blind, implicit and absolute obedience, as that which is properly due to them. And, in a qualified sense, they are some of them very unguarded; others scarce capable of being at all justified; and, in general, all of them do much rather favour of the language and spirit " of after times," than of the age in which Ignatius is known to have lived.

THERE is, perhaps, no fact more notoriously evident, than that none of the sacred writers, nor primitive fathers, either of the same age, or near the same age, in which Ignatius flourished, do hold the least affinity with him, in his strange talk (if it be his) about the officers of the christian church.

If

If we look into the "Paftor of Hermas," the "epiftle of Polycarp," or any other genuine piece, near the time in which thefe epiftles are faid to be wrote, we fhall find in them all the difcoveries of a quite different fpirit. Thefe unitedly concur in the like plain language; fpeaking of the officers of the church in a manner becoming the fimplicity of the gofpel, and the purity and humility of thofe early days: Whereas, when we turn to the "Ignatian epiftles," the reverfe is clearly vifible through them all; little being here to be feen but fuch high ftrains of language, as are evidently adapted, if not purpofely contrived, to exalt the clergy, and fecure to them all power, reverence and fubjection. And how fhall this be accounted for? Why fhould there be fuch a fignal difference between the manner of writing in thefe epiftles, and all the other extant books of the fame age?

To this it is faid, that the ftile of authors is very different, and the turn of expreffion, in every writer, as peculiar to him, as his countenance or gate: For which reafon, its thought to be no ways ftrange, that the manner of Ignatius's writing is not like that of his contemporaries.

It is readily acknowledged, that the particular turn of language, in different authors, is different, as is pleaded; but at the fame time, denied, that this at all removes the difficulty. For a number of authors, writing upon the fame fubject, may each of them write in his own peculiar ftile, and yet agree in exhibiting the like account. The ftile of Hermas widely differs from that of Clement, as Clement's does from that of Polycarp; and yet,

they

they all lead us to think much the same thing about the clergy; and this, very evidently, notwithstanding they severally express themselves in a turn peculiar each one to himself. And why might not Ignatius, with the rest of his contemporaries, have wrote in his own stile, and yet have concurred with them in a like account of the officers of the church? 'Tis certain he might. And it must be ascribed, not to meer difference of stile, but to some other cause, that he so strangely differs from them.

It is therefore further pleaded, Ignatius was a SYRIAN, and its no other than might be expected to find him writing in a "swelling turgid stile." To which it is easy to reply,

His being a SYRIAN may possibly account for his sometimes barbarous Greek, as well as uncouth compound words peculiar to himself; but how it should account for his sentiments concerning the clergy, as differing from those of his contemporaries, is not so easy to say. For not only is the high language in these epistles, but the thing intended by it, quite different from that which is contained in the other writings about the same age. Ignatius is alone, not in stile only, but in real meaning. Unclothe the metaphors, qualify the hyperboles, bring down the rhetorical strains used in these writings, and put them into simple language, and their true spirit, their genuine intendment, will carry the honor and power of the clergy much higher, than it is carried by all the phrases of all the contemporary writers united together: Nor can a person, who reads the epistles of Ignatius, help having excited in his mind a far more exalted idea of presbyters

byters as well as bishops, than by reading all the other writers, till we come to the third and fourth centuries.

THE plain truth is, there is so little resemblance between these epistles, upon the head under consideration, and the other writings of the same age; and, I may add, so great a resemblance between them, and the writings of a POSTERIOR DATE, that one can scarce help thinking, the real author of them was alive in the world, long after the death of the truly primitive Ignatius.

HOWEVER the dispute about the superiority of bishops to presbyters be determined, nothing is more evident, than that the language relative to the clergy, bespeaking the reverence and submission due to them, was very different after the second century, from what it was before. And as the language, in the "Ignatian epistles," is quite different, upon this head, from the language of the age in which this father lived; so it well agrees with that, which was in fact used afterwards.

THIS is particularly obvious, upon a comparison between the books that go under the name of the "apostolical constitutions, and canons," and "these epistles." Before their appearance in the editions of Usher and Vossius, the agreement between them, not in spirit only, but in words and phrases, was so observable, that some have not scrupled to say, that they had both one author. That great antiquary, the arch-bishop of Armagh, was clearly of the opinion, that the same hand interpolated the Ignatian epistles, that interpolated the apostolical constitutions;

constitutions; and is somewhat large in offering the reasons of his entertaining such a thought. And since the publication of the new, and (as is tho't) very much purged editions, the resemblance is still visible; so clearly so, that I can't suppose, but prejudice itself will own, there is a much greater analogy between them, in their high descriptions of bishops, and the honor and obedience due to them, than between these epistles, and any other piece that is not of a much later date.

AND what should be the reason of this? Why should the Ignatian epistles be thus different from all the contemporary writings, and so much like those which did not appear till many years after his death? Why should they be wrote with a spirit, and in language, that are well suited to the claims made by the clergy, and the honor and obedience that were in fact yielded to them, not at the time when they were wrote, but LONG AFTER the supposed author of them was gone out of the world? This surely looks suspicious, and is a shrewd sign of unfair dealing some how or other.—To proceed,

III. THE most weighty consideration of all is, the APPROPRIATION of the names, bishop and presbyter, so commonly and certainly to be met with in these epistles. The learned Daille distinguishes this from all his other arguments, calling it " argumentum palmarium "; as well he might, it being an argument that is founded on one of the best and surest rules in criticism, evidencing a pretended genuine writing to be spurious, or corrupted; namely, it's using words in an APPROPRIATED sense, which words were not so used at the time when

when this writing is known to have been penned, but were so used in AFTER-AGES. The greatest critics ever recur to this as the surest test : Nor is its sufficiency, as such, in matters of this nature, disputed by any. In applying therefore this test to the point in hand, let it be observed,

THE words, bishop and presbyter, are, in the "Ignatian epistles", APPROPRIATED terms; not used in a loose and promiscuous manner, but in a sense particularly ascertained and fixed. Bishops are not here called presbyters, nor are presbyters called bishops; but the officers, stiled bishops, are distinguished from those that are stiled presbyters, and, on the other hand, those that are stiled presbyters are, in like manner, distinguished from those that are stiled bishops. And the terms, bishop and presbyter, are the APPROPRIATED ones, pointing out these different church-officers. And this appropriation of the words is not accidental, but runs thro' all the epistles, and all the editions of them, the Usherian and Vossian, as well as those that preceded them. And 'tis so sacred and inviolable, that, in no case, at no time, upon no occasion, is this use of the words departed from. Not an instance is to be met with, where the word bishop is confounded with the word presbyter; or the word presbyter, with the word bishop : But these terms are accurately and religiously applied to different persons, in a fixed and appropriated sense. That is the manner of diction in these epistles, "obey your bishop, and the presbytery." — "I have been judged worthy to see you by Damas, your bishop; and your presbyters, Bassus and Apollonius."— "The bishop presiding in the place of God, your presbyters

presbyters in the place of the council of the apostles." — "Let all reverence the bishop as the Father, and the presbyters as the Sanhedrim of God." — "Attend to the bishop, and the presbytery." — But I have no need to multiply citations here. 'Tis the very thing pleaded, in favor of episcopacy, that Ignatius ever distinguishes bishops from presbyters. This he has been said to do (if my memory don't fail me) thirty-six times: Which, I am satisfied, is not an enlargement; tho', I must confess, I have not been so curious as to adjust the precise number.

WHAT agreement now is there between the supposed Ignatius, and his contemporaries, upon this head? Do they likewise use the words, bishop and presbyter, in an appropriated fixed sense? The plain answer is, they do not. Far from so doing, they differ as much from him in their use of these terms, as they do from any of the writers of the third or fourth centuries: Nor is there an author extant, that wrote either before Ignatius, or at the time when he wrote, or even afterwards till we are got into the third century and onwards, that uses these words as he does, in a sense so certainly, so commonly, and so invariably fixed and determined.

IT is plain, there is no manner of affinity between the apostolic, and Ignatian use of these words; tho' Ignatius was personally known to, at least, some of the apostles. With HIM they are always appropriated terms; but with THEM, they are promiscuously used, as may be seen in the foregoing discourse. It evidently appears from hence, that bishop and presbyter were not yet settled names

names, signifying distinct officers. And this, as Daille says, was the unanimous opinion of the ancient fathers, who speak of the use of these words in this primitive age. And Dr. Whitby, an episcopal writer, affirms the same thing; as was observed in the discourse to which this is annexed. Nay, Bellarmine himself, a Roman-catholic writer, representing the sense of the fathers upon this point, says, as he is quoted by Daille, "In the apostolic times, the names, bishop and presbyter, were common to all the priests, both to the greater, whom we now call bishops; and to the less, whom we call presbyters." I don't bring these testimonies by way of proof, that these names were thus used in the first age; but only to show, that this tho't of the matter is not confined to those, who live in these latter days, and may be suspected of prejudice against the order of bishops; but that it was the opinion of the ancient fathers themselves, even those of them who flourished after episcopacy took place, and were hearty friends to this kind of government in the church.

And as these names are promiscuously applied in the apostolic writings, so are they in the other writings before those of Ignatius. In Hermas's "Pastor" the word, bishops, is explained to signify * "those that preside in the church"; and those that preside in the church are the † "presbyters that preside in the church". And in Clement's "epistle to the Corinthians," the same officers that are called "presbyters," are expresly spoken of as "cast out of their episcopacy." ∥

* Apud " Apost. Pat. Coteler, " pag. 123. Simil. ix. cap. xxvii. † Ibid. pag. 78. Visi. II. cap. iv.
∥ Ibid. pag. 173. cap. xliv.

And if we turn to Polycarp, the supposed collector of the " Ignatian epistles," and the next and nearest writer to him, he says nothing from whence it can be gathered, that bishop and presbyter were, in his day, appropriated terms, and applied, as such, to distinct officers in the church. Presbyters and deacons are the only officers he speaks of; and he undoubtedly means by them the same church-officers that are called by Clement, and by the apostle Paul, in his epistle to this same church, bishops and deacons. And 'tis remarkable, Polycarp no where uses the word bishop, nor does he say a word of the bishop of Philippi, much less of his distinction from the presbyters of this church: Wherein he widely differs from Ignatius; which is really unaccountable, considering how lately Ignatius, under very extraordinary circumstances, had wrote his epistles, and how particularly acquainted Polycarp ( as is pretended ) was with them; especially considering still further, that Ignatius had wrote one epistle to Polycarp himself, and another to his church at Smyrna, in one of which he " pawns his soul for them that were obedient to the bishop and the other clergy "; and, in the other, makes the bishop so necessary, " that no administration could be valid without him, but whatever he should approve would be pleasing to God."

No more is to be seen of an appropriated use of the terms bishop and presbyter in Justin Martyr, than in Polycarp. Irenæus frequently uses these terms, but in the loose and promiscuous sense; as is well known to all who have read him: Nor do the terms appear to be appropriated ones, till towards the close of the second century; and even then

then the appropriation (as was obferved in the foregoing difcourfe) was not fteadily fixed. We muft get into the third century, and the middle of it too, before we fhall find it, after the manner of Ignatius, facred and inviolable.

UPON which the enquiry is obvious and juft, how comes it to pafs, that Ignatius fhould CONSTANTLY ufe the terms, bifhop and prefbyter, not in the fenfe, in which they were ufed, in the age in which he wrote, but in the fenfe in which they were ufed in OTHER AGES, LONG AFTER HIS DEATH? This ought certainly to excite our jealoufy, and put us upon caution left we fhould take fome knavifh impoftor for the worthy and primitive Ignatius. Words, we know, often vary in their meaning; and fometimes particular words are as fure marks of fuch a particular age, as particular garbs or fafhions. And this is the cafe here. Before the days of Ignatius, about the time of his flourifhing and dying, and for fome confiderable time afterwards, the words, bifhop and prefbyter, were UNAPPROPRIATED terms, and promifcuoufly applied to the fame perfons: Whereas, towards the going out of the age in which he lived, or rather the coming in of the next, they loft their promifcuous ufe, and became APPROPRIATED terms, and were as fuch applied to different perfons, who were accordingly now diftinguifhed from each other by being fpoken of under thefe names. And as thefe names, in the epiftles afcribed to Ignatius, in their pureft editions, are ever ufed in the APPROPRIATED fenfe, diftinguifhing bifhops from prefbyters, we are prefented with a moft evident mark of time POSTERIOR to that, in which the true Ignatius is known to have lived.

ENOUGH

ENOUGH, I trust, has now been said to answer the design I had in view, which was to justify those who pay no great regard to what is bro't from the "Ignatian epistles," in support of episcopacy. And I would flatter myself, that even our opponents, while they judge impartially, will not think, we herein act as tho' we had nothing to say in vindication of ourselves. Bigotry itself must confess there is good reason, at least the plausible appearance of it, to suppose, either that Ignatius did not write the epistles that are ascribed to him; or, if he did write them, that they are handed down to us so MINGLED WITH CORRUPTION, as not to deserve a reception as his genuine works.

---

THE reader is desired to correct, with his pen, the following errata, and such other as he may observe, which have escaped the author's notice.

Page. 10, line 2, read there. P. 15, l. 3, from the bottom r. describing. P. 25, l. 18, read constituted. P. 37 l. 15, r. confessus. P. 39, l. 9, from the bottom, r. confessus. P. 72. l. 5, of the note at the bottom, r. L'arroque. P. 76, l. last, r. confessionum. - P. 77. l. 3. from the bottom r. universali. P. 79, l. last but one, r. or. P. 82. l. 4, del. of.

www.ingramcontent.com/pod-product-compliance
Lightning Source LLC
Chambersburg PA
CBHW020137170426
43199CB00010B/776